ROCK ART

A VISION *of a* VANISHING CULTURAL LANDSCAPE

. . . .

JONATHAN BAILEY

With Essays By: Lawrence Baca, Greg Child, Andrew Gulliford, James Keyser, William Lipe, Lawrence Loendorf, Lorran Meares, Scott Thybony, Paul Tosa

Barry —
Words fail as I try to express my gratitude for sharing your years of desert exploration with me. All I can say is THANKS. You ROCK!

Barry, you have been a great man and guide — I've learned much from this trip. thanx — Barbara Ann

Johnson Books

BOULDER

Published by Johnson Books
a Big Earth Publishing company
3005 Center Green Drive, Suite 225
Boulder, Colorado 80301
800-258-5830
www.bigearthpublishing.com

Cover design by Jonathan Bailey
Text composition by D.K. Luraas

9   8   7   6   5   4   3   2   1

Library of Congress Control Number: 2015948285
ISBN: 978-1-55566-465-7

Printed in Korea

Contents

Acknowledgments

This project would not be possible without the support of: Aaron Goldtooth, Connie Massingale, Diane Orr, Larry Ruiz (Cloudy Ridge Productions), Jim Keele, Celia Sullivan, Alan Cressler, Debbie Wayland, Brad Lewis, Richard Krause, Ecoflight, Jane Pargiter, Geoffrey Smith, Thomas Luebben, Terri Martin, Timothy Riley, Aaron O'Brien, Matthew Aspros, Tim Peterson, Jennifer Huang, Jerry Spangler, Taylor McKinnon, Ray Bloxham, Ryan Hermansen, Bethany Ebling, Joe Pachak, JR Lancaster, Ann Licater, the Utah Rock Art Research Association, USU Eastern Prehistoric Museum, all of the contributors to this book, and, most importantly, my publisher, Johnson Books for sharing and sustaining my vision of conservation.

Introduction

I was born in the San Rafael Swell between pillars of stone, following a topographic map that my parents had given me as a gift. Already it was frayed and crumbling back into dust. I was six years old and eager to taste beyond the insincerities of marked trails and tourist destinations. I wanted something real.

I knew there were wild places, or so I had been told. But I feared that this, too, was a gimmick—something to bring the visitors and their paychecks. What was left of wilderness? I was afraid of asking this question but couldn't resist weaving my life in a search of the answer.

I was too young, as I had been told, to walk the distances that I asked for, but I persisted. This was to be my birthday gift and I would settle for nothing less than the truth.

It was a February morning as we left. I was wrapped in a wool coat and a plaid blanket that my grandmother had woven for my birthday. I was glued to the narrow window of our half-cab in the back seat looking into the canyons that poured back into the earth after miles of meanderings. I couldn't see any cities, roads, or any sign of human occupation. My vision was unobscured. My map told me that the nearest object of human construction was Interstate-70, forty-something miles to the south.

I leaped out of the vehicle as we rolled to a stop at the "Indian Trail," as my map titled it, a narrow and winding entrance into a perennial spring-fed stream and the redrock towers that enclosed it.

I, of course, had my eye on something else—an unmarked, untitled stain on the map indicating a place with no name—a canyon that hadn't been touched, at least, not by surveyors. Before entering, I had to follow the Indian Trail into the main tributary first, as my canyon lie on the other side.

The Indian Trail proved to be not much of a trail at all—to humans, anyway. I had seen several desert bighorn sheep cascade across the ivory sandstone, plummeting down into the brilliant ochre-red walls. The pathway was remarkably steep, too steep, in fact, for my small gym shoes. I stumbled frequently but eventually found myself next to the creek flaked with sparks of amber.

From here we walked several miles west, regularly wading across the waterway. I was small—and cold—the ice-laden water was chest-deep. "Would you like to turn back?" they regularly asked. "No" I always responded.

At the confluence of my canyon with the main tributary a large pool had collected. Cobalt blue marked its depth. Five feet? Ten? Twenty? One couldn't know. Crawdads and sucker fish regularly tested the surface, only to sink back into the darkness.

Water cascaded into this pool from my canyon, fracturing its rhythmic face into four intermittent falls underlain by a variety of striking neon mosses.

We skirted along the cliff wall on the west side, utilizing a small ledge that circumnavigated the pool. From here, the walls were pitted and convex—a blue-gray esophagus by which dried fern leaves clung to life on its upper reaches. On its floor I spotted a brilliant piece of jasper—blood-red and woven with charcoal-black veins. I held it lovingly in my palms as its contours suddenly began to take shape. It was the bottom half of a projectile point—the first I had ever personally found. I questioned who had made it and when. At that time, that answer was as distant as the centuries between me and its maker. I placed it back into the sand and continued into the heart of wilderness.

How far had we walked from the vehicle? Five miles? Ten? Distance didn't seem to matter to me anymore. I inspected every niche and cranny that I was capable of for several miles until something irresistible came into full view—a completely repatinated cliff wall, mirroring layers of sandstone tinted maroon to indigo. I jogged to its face, examining the pockets that were obscured from the canyon floor. The surface was neatly adorned with prehistoric carvings, or, *Indian writings* as we were taught to call them in Emery County. How many people had seen these? I wondered. Just the creator and myself? Or had someone else passed this way?

It was getting late. If the sun didn't tell you that, the temperature certainly did. I suppose we turned back at this point but my memory of it remains foggy, at best. I don't recall ever turning around. I stayed. Didn't I? I never left wilderness. I couldn't have.

***

I woke against the floor of Ivory Canyon fifteen years later with the debris pressed against my cheek. Nothing was spared. The walls were choked with signatures, bullet holes, and the empty sockets where the petroglyphs had been scraped from the face. A recently pioneered ATV trail dissected the canyon floor. No, this was not just a loss of an antiquity. This was the death—the murder—of a life I knew so well.

I began this book several years ago when the destruction had accelerated. By now, it is critical. Sensitive sites are being vandalized, looted, and developed by the masses. Take a careful look. It may be your last. Hell, many of the sites we had originally scheduled to publish as pristine were completely destroyed before we could publish this book.

I applaud all of the acclaimed writers, artists, and leaders who are standing with me in this effort: Lawrence Baca, Greg Child, Andrew Gulliford, James Keyser, William Lipe, Lawrence Loendorf, Lorran Meares, Scott Thybony, and Paul Tosa. Hopefully together we can illustrate that the value of cultural resources is not limited to what the images represent or statistically where they are conceived, but extends into a cultural landscape—into a space imbued with meaning and spiritual dignity; not only to us, but to their creators. The experience of place matters, not only to science, but also to our sensibilities. If we don't preserve that, we don't deserve the land we walk on.

Passage Through the Spiritual Birthplace of the Sacred

Lorran and Charlotte Meares

Piercing the limitations of historical 3D techniques, Meares' photographs have earned him international recognition and inclusion in numerous exhibits, publications, and television shows, including The Macmillan Biographical Encyclopedia of Photographers, Artists, and Innovators; *NBC* Nightly News with Tom Brokaw; Sacred Places: Native American Sites, *with an introduction by Pulitzer Prize-winning author Scott Momaday; as well as being the first solo photographer for a Sierra Club calendar since Ansel Adams. Meares' work advocates for the environment and calls attention to the loss of indigenous sacred places and cultural heritage. Over decades, Meares has collaborated with the Department of Interior, state parks, Bureau of Land Management, archaeological organizations, and Native American tribal groups on projects documenting endangered or vandalized archaeological sites. Meares' images can be found at www.Enlight-10.com.*

One doesn't see as many moons as I without having been touched by the journey that is both my vocation and avocation. Photographing people can be a way to peer—even for a moment—into their souls. But it's *place* that is sacred, because it resonates with and informs the psyche, flays open the mind, and reveals the soul's cosmic dimension.

Transformative space can be breathtakingly beautiful, or shatteringly brutal, but even though we've separated from it physically, it never leaves us, taking residence in the niches and nooks of our spiritual awareness.

Such a place for me is a simple, though profound, rock-art panel—the birthing petroglyph. The terrace, or ledge, upon which its maker stood rises perhaps a thousand feet above the twisting, gnarly, river-carved canyon and valley floor. Pecked and pocked into a slick-as-chalkboard, sheer sandstone cliff, its desert varnish, dark red like eons of dried blood, is the image of a standing woman giving birth. The upside-down newborn, with its fine, feathery hair, emerges into this world and completes the chapter, the cycle, begun by the telling adjacent figures of a man and woman embracing, engaged in face-to-face lovemaking.

The intercourse of time with generations of peoples traversing southeast Utah also births a destruction and exploitation, abuse by those whose innate respect for the sacred in the landscape was a seed that never germinated, or that withered and died.

Reaching this delicate and pristine panel takes time and patience, like the gestation period of the women who first and thereafter painstakingly reached this spot. Good thing, too, because remoteness may be its only salvation—its best defense from the ravages of graffiti, vandals, or the woefully ignorant and disconnected.

A platform to another world, a huge, nearby sandstone slab faces the sky, its lamp-black ancient patina a glistening two-dimensional rock-hard canvas. The hoof-prints of a deer and bear and mountain lion paw prints track across its surface in the direction of a cleft in the nearly touching cliff.

More bear and mountain lion paw prints share this storybook page as a stick-figured Kokopelli plays his flute to the spirits inhabiting the vertical crack behind a triangular-shaped rock. In Native American creation stories, cave openings, rock cracks and crevices frequently represent the entrance to another dimension, or an entrance to the underworld.

The Four Corners hoards a rich cache of the known-world's mystical signs and symbols. Here, in this place, wondrous petroglyphs depict a truly triumphant victory in humanity's story. I've been told that generations of life began here, and the assemblage of information and celebration of rock writing and ritual coalesces at this spot.

I've crawled into that womb-like chamber tucked discretely beside the slab, its niche just large enough for a woman in late-stage labor to rest on a cushion of juniper boughs, monitoring with anticipation the ever-increasing contractions that herald the ritual. The sacred cycle has begun.

Of the myriad rock art sites that I've visited, this one has captured my imagination the most. Perhaps the infant in the portrait—with its full crop of long, straight hair so carefully incised—was destined to become a leader of his people, or perhaps a future mother and powerful clanswoman. The storyteller left clues that make me think this rock writing marks a special birth, not only the specialness *of* birth.

Just above the mother's head, a quail-egg-sized dimple, a half-moon-shaped pocket formed naturally during the genesis of the sedimentary layer itself. The storyteller responded to that celestial inspiration by flaring at least a dozen horizontal feet from that small crater, a pecked serpentine sine-wave. Was this the fiery trail of a star falling, the vaporous remnants of a sky-traversing comet? Mystery remains, reminding those who came after of the spirit energy that once (and forever?) blessed this sacred space.

Within the imaginings of this twenty-first-century art maker rises a celebration of celestial proportions. I sense something deeper than a how-to diagram here. I want to imagine that the intertwined figures coupled in sexual embrace represent the flesh and blood beginnings of this timeless child. Yet, the mystery tugs: life comes from somewhere that is not this world and leaves it for the beyond, the inaccessible space that is hinted at in the shadows of cracks, of tears in the veil between spaces.

Was this dream of fecundity translated through the sacred union of the Sky God and Earth Mother? Perhaps, they also conceived me. I brought my first-born son to this place. It was here that I told him that he, too, was conceived in a dream.

It's rumored that anarchist Edward Abbey visited this very spot many times for inspiration, for wild imaginations, for dreamings, perhaps for the foretelling contemplation of his untimely passing.

Abbey *felt* the "crags and pinnacles of naked rock, the dark cores of ancient volcanoes, a vast and silent emptiness smoldering with heat, color, and *indecipherable significance,* above which floated a small number of pure, clear, hard-edged clouds. For the first time," he wrote, "I felt I was getting close to the West of my deepest imaginings, the place where the tangible and the mythical became the same."

Somewhere, miles from here, in an unholy landscape of cement and steel, in a room of windows that admit no air, the tangible manifests in the personage of the nihilistic Corporation, and the mythical is that delusion that sacred places can survive unregulated and unchecked exploitation. Coal and uranium mines, oil and gas exploration and fracking the hell out of the sacred *Terre Mater,* widening the chasm between the sacred and the profane.

Mircea Eliade, stretching for meaning beyond Emile Durkheim, exposed our dual views of experience and the desacralization of nature and unclothed the impoverishment that results. Was he correct in believing that "No modern man, however irreligious, is entirely insensible to the charms of nature"?

What lies *beneath the surface* of these layered sandstone formations is more than geologic in nature. It's vast fossil fuel resources that send chills up the spine, not a sense of the mysterious. As one-dimensional CEOs plot two-dimensional corporate profit charts to reflect quantitative natural resources, others engineer three-dimensional constructions to probe, drill, scrape, inject, extract, transport, and refine the products of a profane and materialistic imperative. It's a trade off: destruction of sacred lands within the Colorado Plateau for its resources, or preservation of places that for many tribal peoples are the entrance to the immeasurable "wealth" of a fourth dimension.

Koyaanisqatsi: Life Out of Balance, the first in the *Qatsi* trilogy of films by filmmaker Godfrey Reggio, is a tone poem without dialog or narration. Reggio explains, "It's because, from my point of view, our language is in a state of vast humiliation. It no longer describes the world in which we live."

Without words, we're challenged to remember our beginnings—visualize the DNA from which we all come, synchronize and harmonize the relationships among nature, humankind, and technology. With the passing of this Fourth World (of the Hopi and other Puebloans), the earth will be raped no more, its lifeblood no longer sucked away, and a new world will be birthed, maybe, just maybe, without the beings who understood the former ones not at all.

The storyteller's words, the poet's choreographed phrases, the composer's symphonies showcase the brilliance of human creativity and potential to captivate us for many generations. But the often enigmatic, sometimes modest stories, dreams, visions, and, perhaps, warnings, carved as symbols into the sandstone of Utah's grand storybook will remind us we are but sojourners … and stewards.

We visit these special places to be reborn, find peace, understand the interconnectedness of all things, stop the world, restore balance. We go there and find our spirit captivated by enigmatic markings on stone. Seduced by the song of Kokopelli's flute, we're led again and again into a place for which there is by definition no canvas surface.

Creating interpretive and documentary images of this and other sacred places imprinted upon my being an elemental truth, a fundamental law of nature. Abbey's disciples—I among them—sense, if not wholly comprehend, that the sacred landscape holds our history as assuredly as does the cosmos from which we are born.

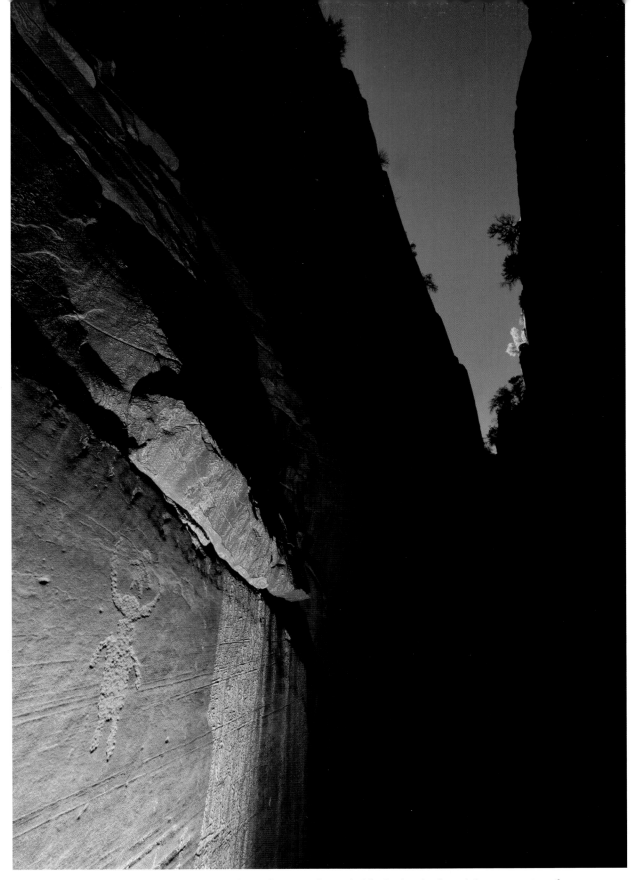

Entrances, tunnels, and crevices became sacred places of origin and a symbol for birth, rebirth, and the regeneration of resources. This petroglyph reflects this environment, portraying a child between the horns of a powerful figure.

The male and female forms unite in sexual union—aligned and shaped to the landscape in which they were placed.

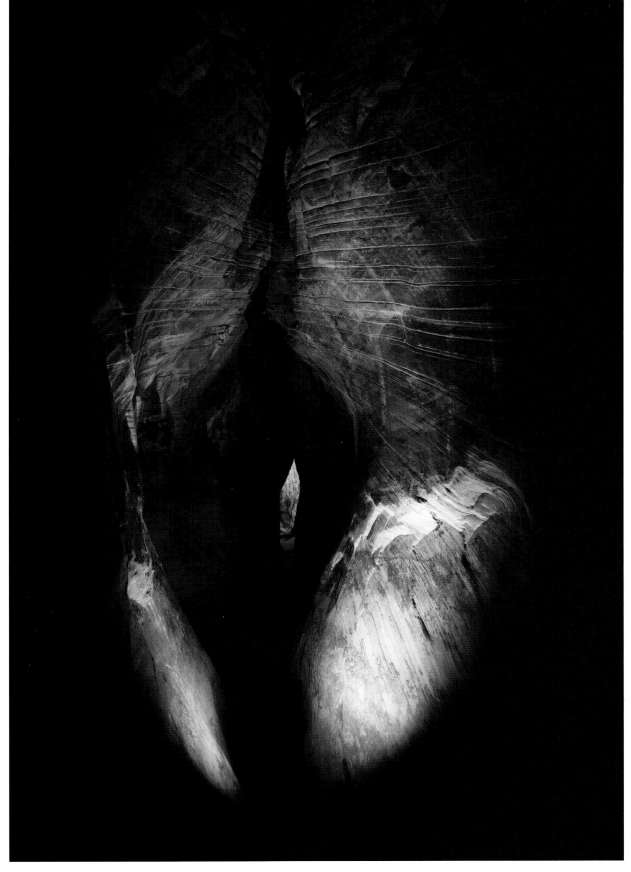

The landscape flows with metaphorical patterns, shaping how we exist within and experience wilderness.

This image is a part of a chosen landscape with a linear alignment of sacred sites and places—each visible throughout all locations in the sequence.

Characters, symbols, and scenes are often found in association with the silhouettes on the horizon. These two-dimensional pictographs and petroglyphs emphasize the four-dimensional landscape, becoming powerful tools to enter the mind and spirit of the individuals who were witnesses to this space.

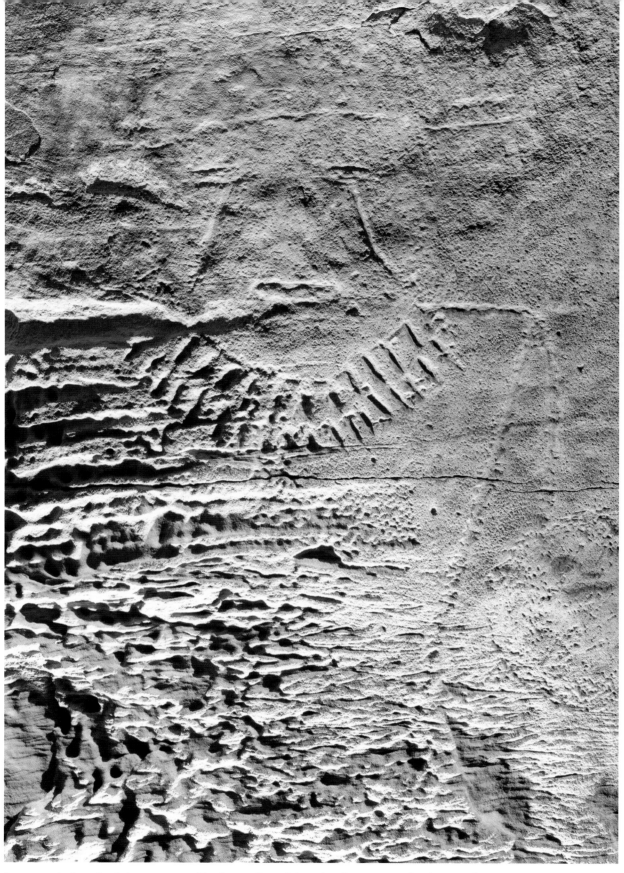

Images can be brutally obvious or impossibly obscure. Some fade within the patterns, subordinate to the textures of the rock itself.

I enter a womb within stone, staring into the eyes of the spirits. My whispers fill the narrow chamber, emanating, not from myself, but from the images. The acoustics embedded into place and stone allow us to resurrect the living past.

A canyon blanketed in fog preceding a flash flood.

Not all granaries are on high, inaccessible cliffs. Many choose camouflage and obscurity over inaccessibility.

To life, water is pure seduction. No matter the quantity or the quality, it is an ecological magnet. I have spent weeks at a time—months perhaps—discovering its breath of life in the deserts of Utah, never being the first. The sandstone surfaces are stained black from ancient organic residues, the walls and alcoves decorated with images carved or painted by distant hands.

Life is dependent upon finding water. Monsoon season brought a blessing—caches of water hidden in niches in the landscape. In the creation of life, it also brought destruction, breaking apart stone and obscuring visions of the past through erosion and staining.

The construction of Interstate 70 has left a sterile experience for the petroglyphs that line this fertile valley.

The infrastructure induced by oil and gas development terrorizes the fourth dimension, robbing the fundamental experience of a cultural landscape and introducing a plague of vandalism due to increased access.

Half of this panel fell in the mid-1900s. Only one photograph is known to exist prior to the natural exfoliation.

What Do We See When We Look at Rock Art?

William D. Lipe

William D. Lipe is a Professor Emeritus at Washington State University and a Trustee of the Crow Canyon Archaeological Center. He has worked in archaeology in the Four Corners since 1958 when he was hired as a crew chief on the Glen Canyon Archaeological Project. Since then, he has become one of the most respected scholars in southwestern archaeology. From 1995–1997, he was President of the Society for American Archaeology. In 2010, he received the Alfred Vincent Kidder Award from the American Anthropological Association for achievement in American archaeology. He has published numerous articles, many of which have become cornerstones for southwestern archaeology.

Humans live in social groups and create "cultural common worlds"—stores of knowledge and meanings that extend beyond the capacity of any individual to maintain. Both language and nonverbal means of communication and representation enable individuals to tap into and to contribute to this common world. Although language is essential to our human way of communicating and remembering, we also build meanings into our physical surroundings, which, over the history of our species, have become increasingly populated with structures and objects that humans have constructed.

Humanity's ability to store and share knowledge has been vastly increased through the invention of writing, and quite recently, through media such as video. However, books and television haven't replaced our need to use both our natural and constructed environments as repositories of cultural understandings. After all, we do find our way through our cities by looking for familiar street scenes and buildings, and we expect directions to be physically manifested by permanent street signs. Natural features, too, such as hills, rivers, and the position of the sun, help orient us, whether in rural or urban settings. Natural and cultural features often serve to trigger societal or personal memories that help us comprehend the world we live in—at scales ranging from the societal to the personal. Think of the Gettysburg battlefield or the plaza in Dallas where John F. Kennedy was shot.

Or the table where our family gathered for meals when we were children.

When we visit archaeological sites in canyon country we are seeing fragmentary physical expressions of the lives of people who inhabited social and cultural worlds very different from ours. But, like us, they also created cultural landscapes that made tangible some of the shared understandings that gave direction and meaning to their lives and that linked them together as members of a community. Names and stories must have been attached to these natural features. Shrines, trails, and the arrangement of living spaces and symbolic features in buildings must have given physical reality to religious beliefs and to patterns of social life. These understandings would have been abundantly expressed in speech, but spoken words fade away immediately, while the physicality of the cultural landscape persists.

Rock art must have played a special role in the cultural landscapes of the past. It is not writing, in that it is not a physical representation of language. However, it is less constrained by function apart from visual communication than is, say, a pueblo building that people live in, or a decorated pottery vessel that also has to hold water. Rock art is free to express a greater range of intended meanings, and often multiple levels of meaning. That makes it harder for those of us from dramatically different cultural worlds to interpret. The handprints on the cliff wall seem merely to say, "I'm here! I exist!" but were they intended to say more? What about the square-shouldered figure with a headdress, neck ornaments, and a belt or kilt—does it represent a deified ancestor or a shaman—and what specifically do the bodily accoutrements signify? Does depicting

a bighorn sheep just reflect its importance as a food animal, or did sheep play a role in mythic history or in symbolizing certain kinds of spiritual or physical strength?

Native American descendants of the people who made the canyon country rock art often have greater insights into what was intended by the artists of the past, but still, this depends on a thousand or more years of cultural continuity in how ideas are represented visually. One of the things that has made human culture so successful is that it can and does change as social or environmental conditions change.

Although we will probably never be able to recover all the specific meanings that an artist attempted to express on the rocks in ancient times, rock art will continue to fascinate us because it offers a direct connection, however imperfect, to the individual artists who made it, and to aspects of the collective knowledge and meanings embedded in those artists' cultural worlds. Furthermore, rock art, like other cultural productions, may have played different roles in the lives of people from later periods, down through time. For example, in the Cedar Mesa area, Ancestral Pueblo people in the AD 1100s and 1200s often superimposed new drawings over images from a thousand years earlier—sometimes "editing" the art, presumably to bring it, in some fashion, into their own cultural worlds.

Today, archaeologists and rock art specialists, in a sense, are also appropriating past rock art for their own purposes. We are getting pretty good at defining and recognizing the styles of depiction that characterize various periods of time. Careful comparisons are beginning to allow us to recognize what we think are categories of meaning for various types of elements. Thankfully, present-day Pueblo people are, in some cases, willing to offer interpretations based on their own traditional knowledge and understandings of visual symbols. In addition, we can assume that rock art often was used to designate places of particular historic or ideological importance to the culture of the artists who made it. We are just beginning to understand and seek patterns in the types of places that rock art consecrates—if that is the right concept—and the ways in which shapes and other characteristics of the rocks themselves interact with the depictions, which is another potentially important area of research.

So many of us are, in various ways, making the ancient rock art of canyon country part of our own cultural worlds. Photographers, for instance, whether students of rock art or not, find the images and their contexts irresistible as subjects for making art with a camera. The interpretive stories that the archaeologists and rock art specialists tell have a ready audience, and we speculate individually as to what the images "really" mean. We give names to rock art images and panels, and as we gaze at them, we feel a personal connection to the artists, even though we know we will never know all they were trying to communicate.

Some scholars propose that these symbols, known as waterglyphs, gave direction to individuals by guiding them to sources of water. This image falls outside of the typical archetype as it is represented with a spiral rather than a singular circle.

The character of stone with huecos, niches, and water-sculpted terraces gives dimension to the images exquisitely depicted on their chosen canvas. This site is no longer pristine as of late 2015. The alcove is now reported to have charcoal signatures marring the sacred images. In addition, an adjacent site is now reported to have had horse anchors drilled into the images.

Hands are a direct—almost tangible—connection to the very essence of an artist. We dissect prehistory into innumerable styles and cultures that separate us further from a connection, but hands are a reminder that, despite themes, it was an individual who painted these. Our preconceptions of culture and style can inhibit our ability to see beyond the labels we create, overshadowing the individual and distilling a more complex prehistory.

There are bridges between place despite distance. A site's most critical component may be located hundreds of yards, or perhaps miles, from the site itself. This incised image is created above a small aperture that has been altered—narrowed for precision—in the prehistoric past by slabs of rock and mortar. During the winter solstice, sunset light is filtered through this narrow passage, hitting a monolith far on the other side of the canyon (Connie Massingale, private conversation). Near to this monolith, a small structure is built atop a mesa acting as an observatory. From this observatory, on the night of the winter solstice, the constellation Orion rises—born between two large knobs on the horizon. This is one of the most extensive astronomical calendars in the Southwest with many alignments that we may never know, extending farther than we may ever reach. Despite its significance, the monoliths are severely tilted and some have fallen due to cattle that actively graze around and rub against the stones. In addition, oil and gas exploration threatens to permeate this extensive cultural landscape with newly developed roads, pipelines, and rigs.

An effigy, likely adored by the individual who placed it under the elongated, ghostly paintings from an Archaic-era artist. It was left as an offering—a gift—to the sacred images or that which the images appealed to. It was placed just over three thousand years (3065–3230 BP) before I discovered it eroding out of the sand. A special thank you to USU Eastern Prehistoric Museum in Price, Utah, and Timothy Riley for radiocarbon dating the artifact and allowing me to rephotograph its beauty.

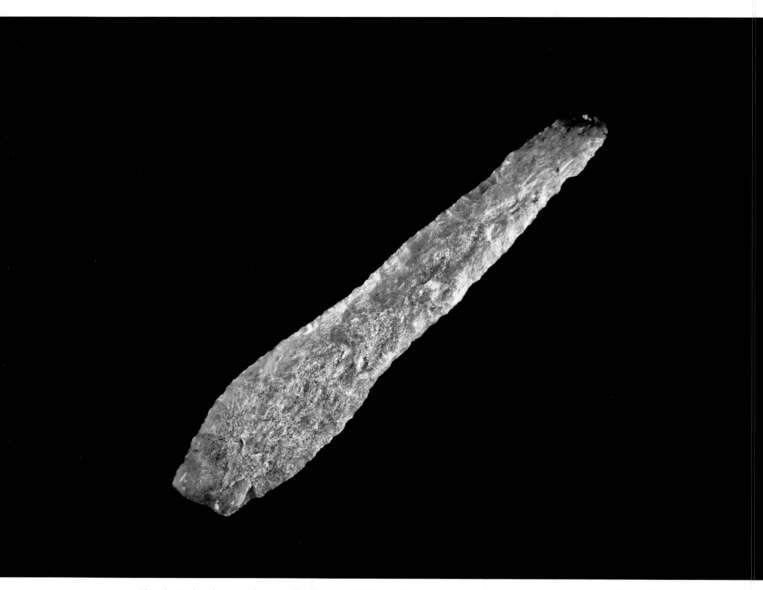

The physical and material traces of prehistoric life bring clarity to the carved and painted counterparts. This knife and petroglyph image (opposite), found nearly two hundred miles apart, are alike in shape, form, and cultural context.

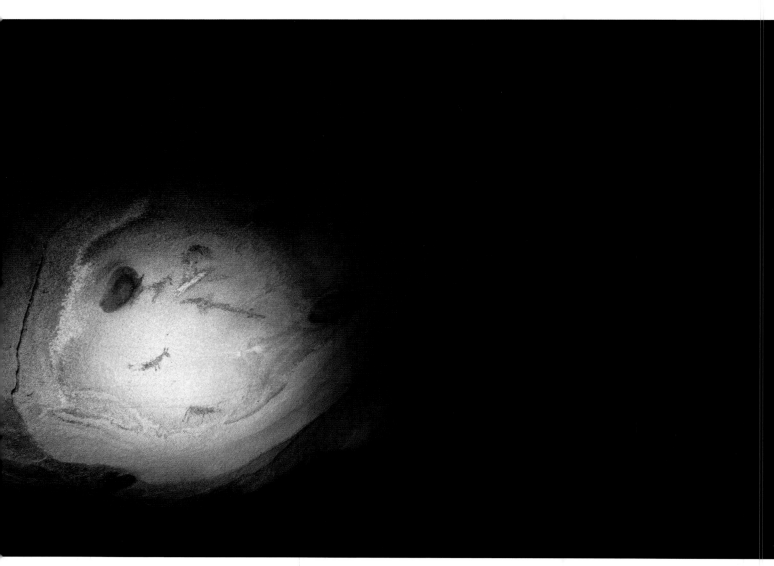

These animal forms, created with the charcoal from a late prehistoric fire, sanctify the interior of a deep cavern, which illustrates an absence of habitation. Here, place is visibly sacred—a space valued much higher than the prospect of inhabiting.

This human figure exhibits an immeasurable wealth of power which, at night, is only illuminated and greatly expanded.

When we think of architecture, we think of utility. We think of the things necessary to sustain a functional and sustainable structure. The value that aesthetics had in the placement and artification of their constructions is neglected and often entirely ignored.

During the night of the winter solstice, Orion rises above this human form, reflecting its shape in stone.

Stories on Stone: Protecting Prehistoric Rock Art

Andrew Gulliford

Andrew Gulliford is a historian, photographer, and Professor of History and Environmental Studies at Fort Lewis College in Durango, Colorado. For a decade Gulliford served on the Southwest Colorado Resources Advisory Council of the Bureau of Land Management. He has received a certificate of recognition from the Secretary of Agriculture for "outstanding contributions to America's natural and cultural resources." He has written many books, including Sacred Objects & Sacred Places: Preserving Tribal Traditions *and* Outdoors in the Southwest: An Adventure Anthology. *He can be reached at Gulliford_a@fortlewis.edu or on his website at www.agulliford.com.*

All night the river roared by. Our rafting party on the Yampa had shrunk to only five clients because of the high water, which at 25,000 CFS meant a memorable June run through one of the quietest canyons of the West in Dinosaur National Monument. That day we had sped downriver making camp earlier than usual. Try as they might, the guides had not managed to land where they wanted to because of the swift water. As we woke the next morning to the rapids' roar, like the sound of furious surf on the Oregon Coast, it became obvious we'd be there awhile. One whole eighteen-foot raft tube lay flat, punctured from the incessant wave action because we'd parked on a sharp rock.

As a Southwest historian and interpreter, my job after breakfast was to educate the guests and to keep them distracted while the guides patched the gaping gash and the glue set up. So we took a hike.

I'd seen a faint red pictograph where a side canyon came into the main Yampa River Canyon and I wanted to get closer. The ledge it was on seemed broad enough to walk on, but not by much. Besides, I had to get our guests thinking about something other than our busted boat. A Class IV rapid lay ahead of us that day and passenger anxiety was palpable.

I thought the pictograph, or painted rock art, might be really ancient, a ghostly Archaic figure that is typically endemic to central and southern Utah. As I described the prehistoric peoples of the plateau to the group, we carefully stepped along the ledge with the river eddying below us. I took a closer look, stopped, and tried not to shout with surprise.

The canyon wall stretched hundreds of feet above us, but just ten or twelve feet higher than we were on the ledge spread an entire panel of petroglyphs perhaps forty or fifty feet long. Covered in dust, lost to time, the red pictograph had been a signal, a sign, of a larger panel unknown in any guidebook. Unknown—as I was to find out—by National Park Service staff.

Thanks to the high water and the popped raft tube, we'd had time for a morning exploration and found something that river runners did not know existed. No one knew about this panel and its warriors, shields, spirals, and anthropomorphs. Because of the clients who were uncomfortable on our narrow ledge and our dangerous position above deep, swirling waters, I could not really study the panel; but it was large and obscured by bright, mid-morning sunlight reflecting off the water and surrounding sandstone. A truly ecstatic find.

The boat was repaired. The patch held. Downriver we went and, later, I contacted the park about the panel and tried to set up a time to go back and clean off this unknown, valuable rock art. Permission denied.

I needed a federal Archaeological Resources & Protection Act (ARPA) permit, and I'm not an archaeologist. Basically, NPS staff wanted it left alone. It had been hidden for centuries, possibly millennia, why uncover it now?

At first, I was angry. I grumbled. I called the park superintendent and got the same answer, but now I'm reconciled. Why not leave it alone and safe from vandals who might walk the same narrow ledge we

did? How do we protect the thousands of elements of rock art found throughout the Southwest? Maybe centuries of dust and dirt are as good a solution as any. If you can't find it, you can't harm it.

I've seen vandalism to rock art that makes a visitor shudder. On the Wolfman Panel, north of the San Juan River, bullet holes deface the wall. Someone took a high powered hunting rifle and shot across Butler Wash at one of the great prehistoric panels in southeast Utah complete with wolf prints, baskets, and one long-distance trader, possibly a *Pochteca*, who may have come from Meso-America. The figure is anatomically correct with carefully etched knees, shoulders, waist, and musculature. It's a striking image with needless bullet holes nearby. "Bubba glyphs" I call the pockmarked holes.

Petroglyphs face threats from vandals willing to damage or destroy rock art, but there are also thieves who try to steal the rock itself. They chip away at ancient panels to remove select figures and by doing so damage the entire site.

In the Mimbres country of southwest New Mexico, the Mogollon culture left extraordinary ceramics frequently looted by grave robbers. Mimbres rock art is distinctive because the Mimbres were willing to etch and carve self-portraits, some drawn carefully enough to illustrate tattoos. I find all rock art compelling but there is a playfulness to Mimbres rock art, matched by the details in their ancient pottery that stylistically stands out. All rock art is distinctive of particular cultures. Mimbres rock art is easily identifiable so I knew what I was seeing when a thief brought in a rock.

As director of the Western New Mexico

University Museum, we were hosting the state archaeological conference. It had been a full day with diverse sessions, group conversations, and interactions among scholars, amateurs, archaeologists, and BLM law enforcement rangers. Everyone had gone downtown for beers and dinner. I was locking up.

I had shut the museum galleries and was in my office when the cowboy brought the rock in wrapped in old rags and placed it on my desk. I tried to tell him the museum was closed and that he had to leave, but then he removed the rags and there, on my oak desk, sat one of the finest male Mimbres portraits I had ever seen. Picasso could not have drawn a simpler, easier profile with the distinctive nose, cheekbones, eye, and hair pulled back and tied in a *chongo* style.

Stunned, I asked him where he got it. He told me it came from a site in the valley between Silver City and Lordsburg. I knew the valley. I knew the site. The artifact definitely had been taken from public land. Shocked, I realized that only a few minutes before I had two or three BLM rangers in the museum who could have easily arrested this man, taken back the irreplaceable rock portrait, and begun an investigation. Now it was up to me to think fast and not alert the cowboy to the deep legal trouble he was in.

I suggested he leave the rock with me along with his name and address so my museum staff could learn more about it. He firmly shook his head "no." He was taking it with him to sell. I had few choices so I said at least give me your name and telephone number in case I come across a buyer. He assented and because I did not have a camera, I quickly sketched the stolen Mimbres portrait. It was that drawing, my hastily written notes after he left, and my testimony that was used against him in a successful federal ARPA (Archaeological Resources Protection Act) case.

Damage to rock art is both intentional and unintentional. Half a century ago the first amateurs, and even professional archaeologists, used chalk on rock art panels to make ancient images easier to photograph and document. Now we know that chalk in the recesses of a petroglyph, just like oils from one's fingertips, can do damage. Furthermore, photographers have built fires below petroglyph panels to replicate evening scenes and to show how stories may have been told at twilight a thousand years ago, but fires and heat can crack ancient glyphs and the smoke and soot can do damage.

How do we visit with respect? How do we maintain public access and also educate citizens about the value of rock art and that scrawling your own name and date on ancient panels is ethically and legally wrong? Clearly, we need a more effective approach in protecting and preserving the ancient past.

During heavy rainstorms, this hunting scene vanishes behind a veil of mud.

Painstakingly painted, these ghost-like human forms likely date back several thousand years. They are depicted high on a small ridge that contours to an undulating vein of a red rock canyon, obscuring their presence from those unaware of its existence. These life-sized figures were composed with a minimum of four distinguishable pigments, which, in an arid and volatile landscape, may have considered the tanks of water that can collect in its environment. The site itself is placed within a spectacular landscape at one of the largest drops into the Colorado River from a plaza of stone protruding from the cliff ledge.

The integrity of this pigment is due to a buildup of sediment that obscures the site from the elements and explorers, protecting the images and the original chunks of ochre used to create the pictographs, which are still found at the site.

The more abstract and entoptic rock art imagery is often easily missed. The patterns, seen within the minds-eye, are well masked within the natural fractures and patterns found within stone.

The landscape is permeated with cultural memory. The mesas were inhabited, the cliffs sustain their spirit, and the creek provided their being.

After this site was rediscovered and published by a blogger and photographer in 2011, a large trail was plowed through the cryptogenic soils around the panel. Literally hundreds of individuals have now visited a site that, before 2011, was virtually unknown to exist. What will the future be for these images?

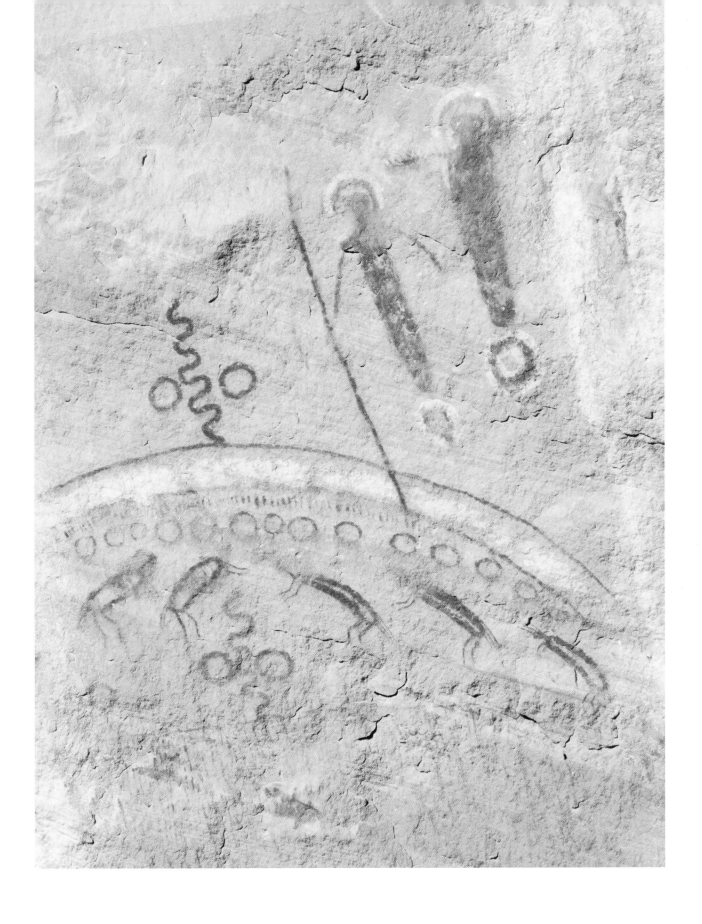

An extremely rare depiction of a monarch butterfly (*Danaus plexippus*) endangered by numerous proposals of development.

Nobody knows the true extent of rock art in the canyon country. It is not typically easy to find or access. Officially, less than 10 percent of public lands have been formally inventoried. This means that permanent land management decisions have to be made without knowledge of the landscape's content.

The situation of a site can influence the mind and evoke deep emotion. This image is located on the lower part of a house-sized balanced rock, which observes an endless sea of canyons below. The two knobs on the head of the human figure reflect its placement in the landscape—mirroring two knobs atop a boulder that obscures the panel. After a blogger discovered this site—although not explicitly revealing its location—ATV trails have been pioneered to the site and large cairns now guide to its location. At this point in time, it seems that it is not a matter of if but when this site will be vandalized. In addition, the site is endangered by proposed oil and gas development.

Local residents of the canyon country have claimed that many rock art sites are recent creations in an attempt to thwart tourism to the area. These false rumors proved catastrophic when a nearby prehistoric pictograph panel was eliminated from the cliff wall by someone who thought it was a forgery.

The "Wolfman Panel" scarred by numerous bullet holes.

This, like many other panels, has seen an increase in vandalism after the first act of desecration. Once vandalism starts, no matter how negligible, it is virtually impossible to stop. It multiplies like a cancer to the site and its landscape.

The Sanctuary

Scott Thybony

Scott Thybony has traveled throughout North America on assignments for major magazines, including Smithsonian, Outside, *and* Men's Journal. *His story on canyon exploration for* National Geographic *magazine was translated into a dozen languages. His books, including* Canyon Country *and* Burntwater *and the* Painted Desert: Land of Wind and Stone *have been bestsellers. The Wilderness Society chose him as the "Voice of the Land" for Grand Canyon National Park, and his commentaries are heard regularly on Arizona Public Radio. Twice the National Geographic Society has awarded him exploration grants, including one to search for Archaic rock art. He once herded sheep for a Navajo medicine man, having a hogan to call home and all the frybread he could eat. You can find his work at www.scott-thybony.com.*

A rattleboard road takes us toward the Lukachukai Mountains and into a cliff-walled region empty of all but a few homesteads. Along the way, we pass a string of sentinel buttes and a dunefield where the sand has migrated, burying a hogan. Even the names on the map have shifted over time, setting us adrift.

With two friends, I'm on the way to meet a Navajo who will show us places he explored as a boy. Tony Williams navigates as I drive, while Scott Milzer stares out the window at the clear skies. Having just flown down from Seattle, he hasn't seen the sun for two months. His last trip to the Southwest was fifteen years ago, so he has some catching up to do.

By mid-morning, rez time, we reach the sheep camp of Vince Benally's mother, set where the branches of a canyon carve back into the mountains. An American flag flutters over her hogan alongside a tree beginning to leaf—a sign that spring has come to the high desert. Our arrival has animated a pack of dogs who surge forward with tails wagging. Vince exits the hogan to meet us while his nephew opens the corral gate to let a dozen sheep and goats funnel out. Today's designated sheep dogs meet the herd and the others climb in the back of Vince's pickup, loaded with water barrels and a bale of hay. We follow it up a sand ridge and deeper into the main canyon where walls of red stone press close.

At the first stop, the Navajo points out a line of hand-and-toeholds angling up a cliff of Wingate sandstone, calling it an escape route. Every bend of the canyon wall reveals another route or a high alcove used as a hideout by women and children seeking refuge in periods of danger. Earlier we had passed a mesa known as Where-the-Women-Cried and a promontory called Massacre Point. The name references an incident during a two hundred year period of raids and counter-raids between the Navajo and New Mexicans.

"They hid the women and children in that cave," Vince explains when I ask about it. "You know how sometimes a bird pretends like it has a broken wing and takes off and you go after the bird? They were doing that. They wanted to get the enemies away from that place, but they found the tracks. They found the women and children there and completely slaughtered them."

We continue up-canyon and stop at a freestanding plug of sandstone called Woman-Walking-Fast-Wrapped-in-a-Shawl Rock. Using binoculars, I scan an alcove high above and spot a masonry wall within it. Next to the ruin stands a white pictograph of a human figure painted in a herringbone pattern. At first, the site appears inaccessible, then I notice carved handholds leading to an upper ledge. Vince says the lower section has collapsed and tries to discourage us, but we decide to take a closer look.

Working up the talus, we reach the bottom of the route, now undercut. After we make several attempts to scale it, Vince steps in and braces himself against the cliff. His nephew turns his ball cap backward, then climbs up his uncle's back and stands on his shoulders. He reaches the first set of handholds and pulls himself up, showing us how to do it Navajo-style. Once a handline is rigged, the rest of us climb the face. This

takes us to a narrow, sand-drifted ledge that we traverse one by one, carefully placing each foot. A misstep would be fatal—or as close to it as you would want to get. Where the ledge ends, we find another pitch requiring a bushwhack to reach the top. With the hard part behind us, we follow a broad ledge to the site. Left back at the trucks far below, the dogs begin to howl. "They miss us," says Vince.

The hanging ruin lies tucked into a pocket streaked with desert varnish. Painted handprints fill the back wall with hues of red and yellow ocher. Laid out in crowded rows, the mass of hands gives an impression of strength in numbers to anyone traveling along the trail below. Mixed in with them are a few triangular-bodied anthropomorphs, a term researchers apply to images with a human appearance. Since no one knows for certain if they portray people or supernaturals, the cumbersome term with a scientific ring to it has come into use. Set off in a niche by itself stands the white figure we saw from below, wrapped in a blanket or perhaps a dress. Up close, it's more difficult to see than from a distance. "You get too close," Milzer says, "and it breaks into pixels." We turn back, and the nephew tells us we are the first white men to reach the site.

A month earlier, a friend took a few of the willing and able to rock art sites he had found in the same area. Alan Roberts, a former climber and x-ray tech, had been making extended trips into the Navajo country for years. During the two days we spent together, I never saw him eat. Not once. With his wiry build, he could pass for an Ancestral Puebloan. That day, we followed him toward the Lukachukais and parked at the end of a series of branching roads. After spending the morning exploring rock art sites, our party returned to eat lunch and regroup.

Holding a chert flake he had found, field biologist Chuck LaRue described its desirable qualities, then mentioned how passionate modern flint knappers could be about good material. "These knappers are just nuts," he said. "They talk about this stuff like they talk about old girlfriends."

We began working out our plans for the rest of the day. Alan mentioned having found a place so pristine he felt as if he were the first person to enter it in centuries. That clinched it. The cliff dwelling we considered exploring could wait, and we set out to find his site. Deep in an unnamed canyon, a steep talus climb took us to the base of a cliff where we entered a hollowed-out chamber sunk deep in shadows. We waited a moment for our eyes to adjust to the dim interior.

The site lay undisturbed as if the passage of a thousand years had barely stirred the dust. Most remnants of the past usually lie buried beneath mounds of rubble, eroded by flash floods, or swept clean by collectors and archaeologists. This place was different. Everything appeared purposeful, nothing haphazard, with all the pieces still fitting. Moving deeper into the sanctuary, we talked in lowered voices in response to the muted light and untracked ground.

Lines of stone running from the back wall partitioned off a portion of the cave below a panel of bold pictographs painted in red and white. Protected from the elements, the images were still saturated with color as if the centuries had only brushed lightly past them. A red figure, appearing to guard the chamber, stood before us with a pair of horns curving downward from its head. Above the guardian ran a red zigzag line, outlined in white, resembling a feathered serpent linked to the sky. Another zigzag below ended at a pair of footprints, connecting it to the earth. Standing inside the chamber, we found ourselves in a world far different from the one we inhabited.

A stillness enveloped the chamber, giving me the impression of a place having been set aside, consecrated. It induced an attitude of respect. In the half light, we continued to search the site, and I noticed a set of three footprints climbing a wall. All had been stamped by a right foot painted white and pressed against the rock surface. The tracks were so clear that I could read the skin pattern, detecting the lines and creases on the sole. Where the rock face met the floor of the cave, the first print was half-buried in the ground as if someone had emerged from below the surface—ghost tracks.

On our arrival, the standard questions had come to mind: who painted these images, how had they affected their lives, and what do they mean? By the time we were ready to leave, they no longer seemed so pressing. I had reached an uneasy truce with the unknown, as those who spend any time in this country must.

The gentle flow of sandstone breathing through veils in time. It is a surface undoubtedly chosen for its spectacular canvas through two distinct eras of carving.

The human brain processes faces to understand origin, emotion, social status, and the health of an individual. Despite its abstract presentation, the faces and masks found in rock art allow us to peer inside and connect to the character of the artisan.

We shape our images with the people and places that shape us. The natural forces embedded into the heart of rock art imagery still exist, unchanged over hundreds, or perhaps thousands, of years. Sharing this unaltered space with a distant hand is a part of a living past—the forces in the landscape that inspired the creation of the images that remain unmarred by the present.

A Navajo *Yeibichai* obscured in a large crevice. During windstorms, the raspy melody of a flute resonates within this cavity due to a series of punctures within the alcove wall.

A sunset before a flash flood in Capitol Reef National Park, Utah—a region with deep prehistory and stunning cultural landscapes.

A magnificent set of images created by an artist several hundred years ago. These images are created with an unmatched precision for their place in time. The largest human figure shown in this photograph stands at only four inches in height and the sheep are equivalent to an inch.

Dinosaur National Monument, Utah, as seen from Point of Pines during sunrise.

Despite their location within Utah, these Plains-like images appear to be Comanche in origin (Lawrence Loendorf, private conversation). This would expand the known range of the Comanche.

69

The birthplace of these images began in place, with a landscape occupied with iron-rich nodules filled with a naturally occurring pigment used to create these paintings.

Rock Art in the Hémish* Landscape

Paul Tosa

Paul Tosa has been the Governor of the Pueblo of Hémes (Jemez) three times and is currently a member of his Pueblo's Tribal Council. He has spent his adult life as an educator and is instrumental in the development of learning experiences for the young of Hémes. Governor Tosa's knowledge of the Hémish landscape and his great skill with the Towa language, spoken only at his Pueblo, create in him the ability and desire to preserve his ancient culture. His grandfather Francisco's gently taught stories of the Hémish landscape are the heart of a book he is writing with Richard Krause titled Eagle Dwelling Place. *Paul lives with his wife, Phyllis, a Hémish potter of note and is surrounded by his three adult children, his many grandchildren, and two great-grandchildren. To him, his family is the inspiration for his keeping the culture of the Hémish alive.*

Hémish rock art is most often seen on U.S. Park Service, Forest Service, or BLM land. Their ancestors inscribed messages near many ancient sites on the Valles Caldera (Wavema) and on the upland plateaus of the Jemez River watershed. Hémish rock art is on other reservations. Trail markers for their migration are on what are now the Jicarilla Apache reservation lands. Some of their sites are within the Zia reservation, while some of Zia's are within the Hémish reservation. In pre-Spanish times, the Hémish took long trading trips to Mexico carrying obsidian from Shiny Rock Valley (Obsidian Valley in the Valles Caldera). They returned with feathers, birds, seashells, and other important ceremonial items. They identified these trails with glyphs along the Rio Grande (Big River) and on their return home, east of the Manzano and Sandia Mountains in New Mexico.

Most outside the pueblo don't know that the uplands of the Jemez River watershed including the Valles Caldera are their ancestral homeland. They have found this landscape to the north of Walatowa sacred since they built many large pueblo villages on the upland plateaus on which they had lived since their migration seven hundred years ago. They were forced to the lowlands by the Spanish in the seventeenth century.

---

*This is our preferred spelling of our mountains and our age-old culture. By using the "H" it rids the name of the Spanish "J." The accent means that the correct pronunciation is like "Hay-mish." There are no other modern place-names in our mountain homeland based upon the names we have given them. Our language is Towa, spoken now only by our pueblo members.

The Hémish continue to have little control over public access and vandalism to even their most sacred places. The National Park Service and the U.S. Forest Service are under pressure to let all who wish to wander freely among them, but they also hold the keys to protecting Hémish sacred places and trails. Unfortunately, the U.S. government, some time ago, established Hémish reservation boundaries without any consideration for the heart of their ancient and sacred places. The Hémish homeland and the reservation bear little resemblance.

—Richard Krause

The Towa name for rock art is *Quasho To'O.* You can translate it into English as "Messages from our Ancestors." As I see these inscriptions on the rock walls, I feel much the same as I do when I walk through the ancestral homes of all who have gone before us in our upland landscape. Our ancestors are there in the glyphs and the ancient villages. In spirit, they are still there in their large, multi-storied, many-room pueblos. I pray for them to grant us health and good crops. I ask them to guide me in the ancient ways.

The Hémish Upland Ancestral Homes

We built our villages and named them for what we saw as important. *Place of the Crow, Where They Hunt Like Eagles, Medicine Bowl, Place of the Flowers, Sea Shell Place,* and many others are in the mountain mesas above our current home of Walatowa. Surrounding the villages were planting-houses and small terraced fields placed so they could capture the moisture that fell on the plateaus.

Thick caps of solid rock define these mesas. These cliffs helped to protect us. These cliffs also gave our ancestors a place to inscribe our symbols expressing who we are even to this day. In the *Quasho To'O* we see our strength as defenders of our

people and culture. In them are our prayers for rain on our crops. In them, we ask for success in hunting. They are the paintings hanging on the walls of our cathedrals. Each one marks a sacred place for me and all the Hémish.

Grandfather Francisco

I moved into my grandfather's living space when I was only seven. I remained at his side as he traveled through our landscape to its most significant Hémish places. I listened to him as we farmed our crops—chiles, corn, squash, tobacco—on the small irrigated fields between our house and the *Large Serpent.* He was a gentle teacher in the ways of the Hémish.

Grandfather's name was Francisco. His Hémish name given him by his parents was *Wah-bakwa* or Medicine Bowl. His parents foresaw something in his life when they named him after the bowl that our healing societies use to prepare their medicines.

Francisco spoke little English, but he knew Towa better than anyone. He was initiated into the Arrow Medicine Society. He was a farmer in the tradition of the high-altitude ancestral farmers who could grow corn in very short growing seasons with little rain. Our ancestors had known how to feed large village populations from the beginning of time. They knew that there was more moisture falling on their small fields in the upland plateaus. They also knew that the grip of winter was there longer, and frost returned earlier than at the lower levels.

Francisco learned to shear and care for sheep in the shadow of *Wavema*, the largest of the resurgent lava domes of the Valles Caldera. I helped him farm and raise sheep. Every night, he sat by his red-hot stove and told me his stories before he went to sleep. He clasped his hands behind his head and pointed in the direction of the place he was talking about with his elbows. All of his stories had a place in our homeland. His stories gave meaning to all we could see surrounding our home. Many stories were about the ancient drawings hidden from the outsider's view.

Grandfather was always telling me the stories of the Hémish. I listened carefully.

We have only one photograph of Francisco, but we have beautiful word pictures that tell us much of who he was. N. Scott Momaday enhanced this one photo in his *House Made of Dawn* and his memoir, *The Names*. "Francisco Tosa" is the name given in *House Made of Dawn* to the grandfather who symbolized the one who has within him the age-old Hemish culture. He also carried the burden of ensuring that it survives. Calling this central character "Francisco" wasn't a naming decision made by chance. Scott Momaday and his family knew our family well. We lived across the dirt road from the Day School where his parents, Natache and Al, came to teach us. They taught us well.

Francisco's task in the novel and in my life was to do all there was to be done to

see that our lifeway, this ancient and lasting culture is learned by the young and sustained by the adults of the pueblo. In this way, he made sure that the Hémish future would flourish in a world that has often sought to dilute or destroy it.

Hémish Rock Art
The Hémish high country landscape has many "messages from our ancestors." I have seen most of them and I am moved every time I go with my own great-grandson, Kennedy, to talk with him about their importance. Among the most significant to us are those that go to the heart of our connectedness with nature. We carry our cornmeal and pollen to honor the images that are so closely tied to us in prayer.

To take the youth of the pueblo to see and feel the power of the messages from their ancestors helps me carry out my task of preserving Hémish ways. A number of the older members who haven't had the experiences I have had are hungry for a better understanding of our landscape as well. We have so many messages inscribed in the rocks and their subjects are many. Grandfather Francisco and I have found three themes irreplaceable and moving to me. Let me tell you about them now.

The Horned Serpent
Throughout the canyons of the Hémish homeland, you will see if you look carefully, the zigzag shape of the Horned Serpent. The Serpent decorates the "kilt" I wore when I danced in the Buffalo Dance in the Walatowa plaza when I was young.

This image signifies water. In some cases, it marks the location of a water source. In others, it is a prayer related to our songs and dances as we ask the clouds to come and bless us with their moisture.

Of course, water was the most vital resource to our ancestors, and to our pueblo's farmers who today cultivate the patchwork of fields to the west of Walatowa. We call the upper reaches of the Jemez River, *The Small Serpent*. As the east and west forks of the Jemez River join, and as the Guadalupe and Jemez come together, we call the combined flows, *The Large Serpent*. As is the case with most of the other rock art of the Hémish, the Horned Serpents are not on our reservation land. Some are very close to public campgrounds.

The Spiral

This motif is often contained within other rock art panels in the Hémes homeland. It may stand alone. The Hémish emergence into this world when it all began is at the center of the spiral. As this rock pattern spirals out, it is both a timeline of the Hémish in this world, and it signifies our culture's endless future.

When I see it, I am reminded of all those who have come before us. Grandfather Francisco taught me that it spiraled on into eternity. If he did his job right, and if I do mine, and those who I gently teach do theirs, then the Hémish people and their pueblo culture will flourish for years to come.

Mother Nature

Connectedness is an important word for us. We are connected to our mountains and to the birds and animals that live in them. We are connected to the plants and trees. We are connected to our ancestors through the pictures they left inscribed in the rocks near the places where they dwelled so we could hear them. The clouds in the sky above us with their life-giving rain are essential to us. Although simple in design, the *Quasho To'O* inscribed what we call Mother Nature. Her image reminds us of our interrelationship with all that lives and grows and stands in our Hémish homeland.

I went to one of my favorite places near the upland ancestral pueblos. It's hard to get to. Not many are aware of it. It involves knowing the right place to come down off the mesa top. Grandfather showed me the exact spot. You then have to scramble across some loose rocks high above the canyon floor. I go there because Mother Nature is there on the cap-rock wall. Her face is mask-like. It has two horizontal eyes to see all and a mouth to symbolize our ancient oral teachings. The mouth is the source of breath that says life to us. We breathe upon our spirit-bowl offerings when we eat. We breathe upon our cornmeal before offering it in prayer. Mother Nature's breath brings life to us.

The rectangular head connected to a rectangular body by two lines that form a neck is one of the best examples that Grandfather Francisco took me to. Sun shines brightly upon Mother Nature on this southwest-facing stone cliff during a summer afternoon.

I hadn't been there in several years.

"There she is," I shouted, only to look closely and see that someone had used this, our Mother Nature, for target practice. Why would they do such a thing? How did they ever find it?

My heart was broken.

There is a point when a site has lost its spirit, when there is nothing left to be experienced but the death of place.

Vandalism has increased over 1,000 percent in the last few years. Rock art remains as the vision of a vanishing cultural landscape.

In a life without balance, we conceive of a past that is replaced by us. Defacing, destroying, and robbing the past has become our way to cope with a reality we can't comprehend—that life didn't begin with us.

I spent some time in basements and attics looking through the photographs and notes from the bygone explorers of canyon country. Images of a vanished landscape were often tucked in forgotten corners—stuck to the sides of old cigar boxes, hidden in personal journals, and obscured by decaying desks. They present a vision of the past—figures that have fallen off of well-known panels, whole sites that have collapsed under the weight of the cliff, and rock art prior to its desecration from vandalism.

Ephemeral space is especially sacred, gracing our memories as a moment of a timeless and vanishing performance.

Stone beads and Tusayan Polychrome ceramics, which allowed us to date the site to about AD 1270 (after this canyon had been mostly abandoned), were stolen from caches near this site. (Jerry Spangler, private conversation). A critical piece of the past was taken from these images.

A figure in a transformed state, holding a serpent up to its mouth as if it is whispering to or drawing the essence from its slithering form. The images were meticulously planned in a reddish-purple pigment, then painted in a bright red ochre.

A nuclear power plant is scheduled to be built along the Green River, a vital lifeline to our prehistoric past. How will that change how we experience and interact with the rock art imagery that embellishes the river?

Place and placement was often much more influential to ancient artists than geographic location. This pictograph is situated on the underside of a large boulder forcing the viewer to lie on his/her back to view it in its entirety.

A small serpent carved onto the side of a slot canyon. Rock art images found within slot canyons are very rare and easily destroyed during periods of flash flooding.

These plains along rivers and creeks were heavily inhabited in prehistory.

Unchanged

Jonathan Bailey

Jonathan Bailey is an artist devoted to protecting cultural resources and the wild landscapes they inhabit. He has covered thirty thousand miles of Utah's backcountry on foot, exploring the art and minds of the people that lived there hundreds to thousands of years ago. He preserves the largest collection of photographs of San Rafael Swell rock art in the world and one of the largest collections of Utah rock art photographs internationally. His award-winning work, in both art and conservation, has been featured throughout the world in well-known journals, books, newsletters, magazines, and television shows. His work can be found at www.baileyimages.com.

The canyons had evolved into a deep blue. The blue of a redrock canyon extinguished by the thirst of night. The cliff walls surrounded me, sinking below me into the Green River, appearing as if it had been painted on the landscape—an aquamarine stroke of the hand.

I followed the measures of stone into a canyon slithering down to the sandstone floor that was stained black from the buildup of bacteria. This place. This landscape. It manifests its austerities in the form of off-chutes—thousands of them— that mark this place with mazes, serpentine canyons, and cavities where an individual could vanish indefinitely. Taken alone, this canyon comes in tides. Inhaling. Exhaling. Obscuring navigation through endless pockets within the earth. I looked down into its middle tier. Into a pool desperately clutching to an array of plants given life by the essence of water collected during the latest pattering of a rainstorm. This is where creation begins: at the face of water.

The water, as I approached it, was tinged with an amber complexion. Perhaps, I thought, it was not water at all; another illusion in a landscape that is absolute. Tadpole shrimp scattered into the corners of the basin, pressing their bulbous bodies against nodules in the pool, quickly vanishing from sight. These shrimp are ancient like the landscape itself—a living fossil that has remained mostly unchanged since the Triassic. This pool has been here forever, it seems, but its conception was less than a week prior to my presence.

The canyon, too, feels unchanged despite the palpable tracks of wind and water. It emptied into large bowl-shaped alcoves pinched together at their far reaches, opening their mouths for consumption. In one of the recesses, I dropped my pack, investigating the hueco-shaped nooks and crannies that blanketed the ceiling. Even in the darkness, the images painted in russet ochres materialized: canines with whimsically curved tails, avians that flocked through layers of stone, and the elongated bodies and ghostly eyes of the human-like forms. Many of these figures appeared far beyond human. They stare back from the beige walls in a transformed state of being, exhibiting the heads of canines and the wings of birds. The intricacy of these images is unmatched, requiring a single-hair brush or, possibly, the tip of a yucca stock. There were no less than sixty images varying from the idiosyncratic processions of desert bighorn sheep to the spectral faces that penetrate the layers of time.

Here, in the empty sockets of stone, time is transcendent—transformative. A corrugation of people. Furrow after furrow. Fold after fold. Reaching back through the creases of time to feel the warmth of the proximity of their past—the heat of ancestors' bodies as if they are expected to return. Will they?

Like the rock art, the languages spoken in this space have woven themselves into the landscape. Abrupt like thunder. Smooth like the pattering of a female rain. They, too, are vanishing from their place in this landscape. With them, they take the stories and beliefs that saturated this space and ingrained the naturally inherent value of the past.

This canyon. This spring. This alcove. They have seen many things. Words have been spoken here in different tongues, in different times. Vibrant words that echoed through these walls like an unsung melody. Images have been tattooed on the flesh of stone, painted, carved, shaped from its raw face. Walls have been raised; four slabs— four plates of sandstone each—pressed together at ninety-degree angles to construct bins for piñon nuts and other gathered foods. Stories have been told here, resurrecting the landscape and their cultural past. The culture. The art. The landscape. It is all one.

Beneath this ground is something much more valuable than oil and gas reserves. On the skyline, there is something much greater than strip mines, shopping centers, and suburbs. The wealth of place is in the layers of knowledge. Not the layers beneath our feet that can be excavated, hauled off to a museum drawer, and "saved" for future generations, but in the layers of canyon country. The layers of cultural memory stitched into place, position, space, and alignment. The layers of meaning—the stories and spoken words; the beliefs and sacred knowledge; the processes and places that confessed their secrets to the people that externalized this wisdom in the creation of these images.

The art is most valuable if it exists without change. The artifacts—the stone tools, baskets, the affectionately buried human bodies—are most valuable here in the place they belong. Development brings a sense of looting—a looting of the spirit, landscape, knowledge, and past for monetary things. The message resounding in the cliff walls, the basins, and the river corridors is clear: "Keep it the same, keep it as it is."

Like the panel's symbols and placement, the turquoise pigment may also be associated with water. Greenish-blue pigments are commonly high in copper, formed in clean air/rural environments due to a chemical reaction of the copper with carbon dioxide and water. Thus, this pigment is more readily available around the flanks of water sources, possibly becoming a symbol for water and/or the production of rain. The turquoise hue is also visually reminiscent of water itself.

Despite this being one of the most recognized and exquisite panels in Utah, it has been marred with several names and chisel marks from those trying to remove the images (out of frame).

I arrive in the morning with slivers of coral hues filtering through combs of ivory sandstone. The pictograph fades entirely most of the day, so I have arrived before the show of light begins. I sit, reflecting the light back to the ghostly figure. It appears out of the rock as if it is walking forward, pulling out of the stone to observe the valley below once again. I am likely the first person to see the image with this level of clarity in thousands of years, and yet I recognize the artist's distinctive methods and icons almost immediately from other panels in this landscape. The figure is bordered on either side with rainbow-like forms and from its hands numerous specks, possibly representing piñon nuts, spiral down into the stone face. For now, it is protected with obscurity.

A human figure painted in a cavern between a fallen boulder and the cliff wall.

The larger-than-life desert trumpet flower (*Eriogonum inflatum*) possibly depicted on an unusual conglomerate cliff wall. This plant was often used as a makeshift pipe for psychoactive agents, emphasizing an ethereal message enclosed within the delicate paintings.

The cliff lines opposite these paintings would fall outside of what is considered a site and thus may not receive protection if development projects were proposed in this canyon. Thankfully, this is not yet a reality we have to face for this panel.

The artification of architecture can easily go unnoticed. Often, these structures contain expert stonework, ornamental mosaics in the mortar (often representing maize or serpentine figures), objects pressed into the mortar or, in many cases, impressions of feet in the mortar (Connie Massingale, private conversation).

In the past, rivers acted as veritable highways—lines of connection through areas thought to be separated and isolated from other regions in the western United States. The remnants of travelers can often be seen along these corridors, complicating our perceptions of the social makeup and ranges of people.

Physical culture often sheds light on the more ethereal remnants of the past, including rock art. Despite the uniqueness of this petroglyph, the shape of the cradleboard allows us to see that this image was likely created by a Numic-speaking artist.

101

The lifeblood of Natural Bridges National Monument below "Kachina Bridge Ruin."

This site is exceptionally unique, executed in a brilliant and exceedingly rare blue-green color, which suggests the presence of copper within the pigment. The panel is endangered by a series of pioneered ATV trails that cross sensitive cryptogenic soils and increase access, placing the site at a high risk for vandalism.

Rock Art as a Landscape

James D. Keyser

James D. Keyser is a respected scholar who has conducted rock art research in both national and international arenas. He is a member of the Science Advisory Committee for the Study of Chauvet Cave and is listed in Who's Who in Rock Art. *He is retired after twenty-seven years as the regional archaeologist for the Forest Service. Prior to that, he was an assistant professor at both the State University of New York at Buffalo and the University of Tulsa. He currently maintains a faculty affiliation with the University of Montana. Keyser has published more than 150 archaeological publications, including:* Indian Rock Art of the Columbia Plateau, The Five Crows Ledger: Warrior Art of the Flathead Indians, Plains Indian Rock Art *(with Michael Klassen),* L'Art des Indiens des Grandes Plaines *(Leseuil, France), and* Art of the Warriors: Rock Art of the Great Plains.

Deep in the Hell's Canyon of the Snake River, on the border between Idaho and Oregon, is the Pittsburg Landing petroglyph site. Pecked on nearly two dozen granite boulders, deposited on this high terrace above the Snake River, and sculpted by the Bonneville Floods some 14,500 years ago, are hundreds of circles, chains, loop lines, dots, zigzags, gridirons, along with a few simple human figures and vulva-forms.

The centerpiece of this rock art site is a dramatically sculpted boulder with a shape that reminds current-day visitors of a Mexican sombrero with a tall peaked crown surrounded by a wide, slightly upturned brim that forms a channel in which water remains for weeks after each rainstorm—sometimes staying full all summer long.

The site is well-known to visitors for this particular boulder, which is fondly referred to as the "Mexican Hat." This ice age sculpture is more than four feet tall and covered by a lightly pecked, interlocking, curvilinear abstract design involving loops, circles, and dots, but it also has two stick figure humans and a lizard carved on the brim. Directly atop the peak of the boulder, the artists pecked three or four cupules, the largest of which has been expanded into a small bedrock mortar more than four inches across and 1.25 inches deep. Where the boulder sits on the ground, small animals have excavated burrows under it into the naturally sculpted hollows that lie just below the surface of the soil.

The petroglyphs at Pittsburg Landing

are a fascinating example of the desire held by prehistoric individuals to leave their mark upon the landscape, but as rock art scholars, we search for deeper meanings in these images by looking at what they depict and how and where these images are placed in the landscape. With such simple abstract petroglyphs—such as dots, lines, circles, and very few simplistic human and animal forms that are familiar to the current-day eye—understanding the content of curvilinear art has always been difficult. So for years rock art scholars assumed that we would have probably never known much about why the ancient artists made these marks, but recent landscape-oriented archaeology has provided us some startling clues (Loubser 2002:69).

The first of these discoveries occurred some years ago on a visit to Pittsburg Landing with a group of rock art scholars. On that visit I was accompanied to the site by a South African rock art expert, Jannie Loubser, whose studies of African sites had included examples painted and carved by both San hunter-gatherers and Bantu-speaking agriculturalists. After looking at the rock art on many of the boulders and concentrating our examination on the prominent "Mexican Hat," Loubser urged the group to take a metaphorical step back from the sculpted boulder and look at it in context. Suddenly, it became clear to all of us; the Mexican Hat, when silhouetted against the dominant mountain on the skyline, shared a very similar profile. The boulder first became that mountain and then became an entire cosmos. It was initially obvious that the artists, who lived year-round in this striking landscape, saw the top of the sculpted boulder as a representa-

tion of the "upper world," which touched the sky like the mountain in the background. The upturned rim, with its water-filled channel, could then be understood to mimic the river and the adjacent "lower world" where people lived year round. The presence of water in this metaphorical landscape, especially in a unique in-the-rock setting, corresponds well to the religious belief system of the Great Basin Indians who believed that metaphysical power resided in such places (Miller 1983:78). Additionally, the hollows under the rock would then represent the caves and rock shelters that were believed to act as an entrance to the "underworld" where the spirits were thought to dwell.

Such a tripartite world division is quite common in the Native cultures and belief systems of this region. The placement of the abstract petroglyphs on this specific boulder could then reflect that division with human figures carved on its "lower world" rim and on top, a cupule expanded into a bedrock mortar (where offerings to the "upper world" would be prepared and left). Here, on this boulder, religious specialists of the past may have carved these images and prepared offerings as part of their ceremonies conducted to petition sacred deities for the renewal of their world.

Having a single example of such a landscape-oriented petroglyph was interesting, but it remained little more than a curiosity for several years until archaeologists discovered similar rock art sites intimately associated with water-created landscapes that bear witness to the same underlying concept of sacred geography. The first of these was Max Pavesic, who noted that prehistoric artists along the Snake River, more than two hundred miles upstream from Pittsburg Landing, had carved their petroglyphs almost exclusively on Bonneville flood-transported boulders (these being basalt boulders called the Melon Gravel) similar in size, shape, and setting to those at Pittsburg Landing. Along a stretch of the Snake River more than one hundred miles long, Pavesic argues that prehistoric artists selectively carved petroglyphs on these water-lain and water-sculpted Melon Gravel boulders because they recognized their origin as being derived from a flood of immense proportions. Additionally, such a flood corresponded both to their world renewal creation story (Pavesic 2007:21–25) and the belief that water (or its effects, like the unique, giant, displaced, water-sculpted boulders) embodies spiritual power. The result is a sacred landscape that derives from the same concept as the petroglyphs at Pittsburg Landing.

At the same time that Pavesic was documenting the sacred landscape of the Melon Gravel, between three hundred and three hundred and fifty miles downstream from Pittsburg Landing, along the shores of the Columbia River, my own research began to document flood-deposited basalt boulders that had been selectively chosen as the "canvasses" for petroglyphs. In the Dalles-Wallula Gap area, there are several key petroglyph sites that were obviously selected because they were flood-deposited boulders (Keyser et al. 2008:20–21), but there are so many other sites in this stretch of river that these do not stand out as a sacred landscape as they do along the upper Snake River.

In the Portland Basin, however, a large cluster of flood-deposited boulders forms a site complex that has much in common with the Melon Gravel landscape. Known as the Effigy Beach complex, these sites include large bas-relief effigies (including the famous "Beaver Bowl") and many flood-rounded boulders covered with cupules (Keyser 2010). However, one of these stands out because its carved features create a metaphorical landscape of miniature "lakes" and "streams" designed to transport water poured into large cupules through a series of carved channels so that the flowing water eventually cascades over the edge of this giant boulder into the Columbia River. Clearly, the movement of water across this carved, miniature landscape was an important part of some ritualistic practices by the inhabitants of the prehistoric village in this area.

For the prehistoric Indian artists of various tribes living along the Columbia-Snake river system, the land was alive with a spirit power that presented itself as a flood-altered landscape of giant, strangely sculpted boulders deposited in unique settings. This sacred geography reflected the cosmos of these people and they marked it with petroglyphs in recognition of its importance to their understanding of how the world had been formed.

During the vernal equinox, a phallic-shaped beam of light penetrates a narrow chamber, which likely acted as a metaphor for a vulva when they were created, crossing the painted figures in procession. This site is endangered by proposed oil and gas development.

In the Book Cliffs mountain range, images of bison are often attributed to Ute artisans. Many of these panels appear to be much more worn, more varnished, and of archetypes found typically in older Formative-era petroglyphs. These images may illustrate that populations of bison were roaming the Book Cliffs in the past.

Flute players painted below a carefully banded cliff wall, flowing like a melody encrypted in stone.

Despite the well-patinated cliff wall behind this site, this petroglyph is carved onto a more challenging rock face, illustrating the significance its placement had to the artisan.

Subconsciously, we use false boundaries to think about the people and places that played major roles in prehistory. Roads, state and county boundaries, townships, and other current-day labels have unnecessarily separated the people and places of the past, including our perceptions of this site in relation to the bigger picture of the region.

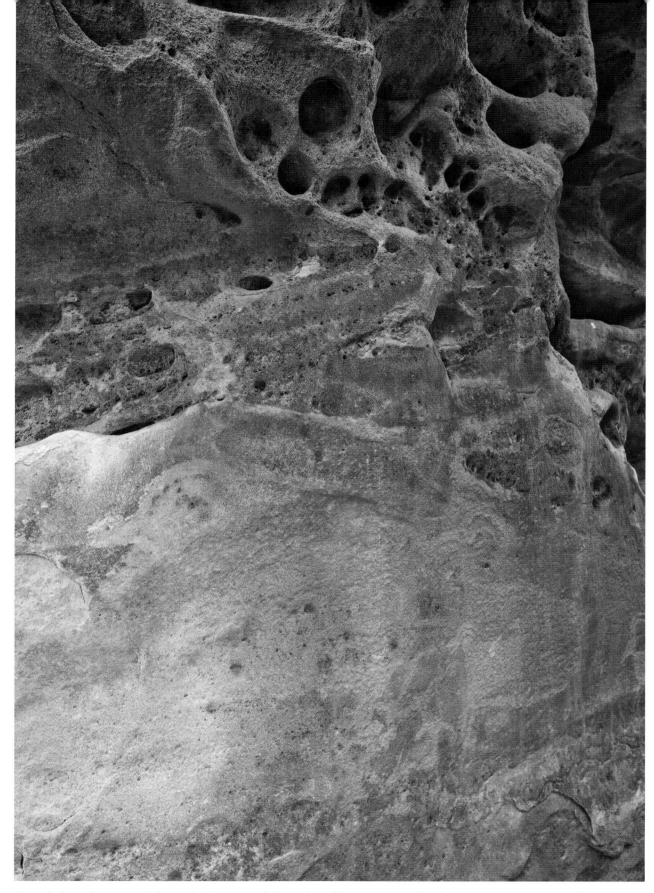

Desert bighorn sheep, created during the Archaic era, fade into bone-like protrusions of sandstone that animate the animals as if they are galloping through stone.

The photographic record of prehistoric rock art is virtually non-existent. When these sites are vandalized or naturally exfoli-ated, we rarely have a record of what it was in the past.

This image is carved above a small niche that may have acted as a shrine to place an offering.

Aerial view of Snake John Reef, Utah, during sunset.

Beyond Seeing the Great Gallery

Lawrence R. Baca

Lawrence R. Baca (Pawnee) is an award-winning attorney who pioneered a legal career championing the civil rights of American Indians. He was the first American Indian hired through the Attorney General's Honor Law Program, the first American Indian president of the Federal Bar Association, and the eighth American Indian to graduate from Harvard Law School. He was the first recipient of an award named in honor of his work from the Federal Bar Association, as well as a founding member of the Indian Trial Lawyer Association in the Department of Justice. In addition to his work as an attorney, Baca has provided a voice for prehistoric artwork through his photographs, written works, and interviews. He retired in 2008 after thirty-two years with the Civil Rights Division, United States Department of Justice.

The 750-foot-high walls will speak to you if you listen. The voices of the spirits in the canyon are carried on the winds with the dust and the scent of the willow and cottonwood trees that guard the Barrier Creek. It is a spiritual place, a place of human silence and emotional resonance.

The Great Gallery in Utah is a panel of painted Archaic-era spirit images two hundred feet in length with over forty major life-size figures, some as tall as eight feet. To me, it is the single most magnificent Native American rock art panel in the United States, but whenever I think about the Great Gallery, I think not only about what is on the cliff wall, but also about the land and the remoteness that has, so far, protected it, along with the high red-brown walls that house the spirits of the ancients who left these images.

When you drive toward the canyon, the land is flat and dry, contrasting the beauty of Horseshoe Canyon that awaits you. From the parking lot, the canyon rim is invisible but the trail to the bottom of the canyon is well marked, well maintained and … well … steep. The last half-mile is a sand hill, which means that when you return to your vehicle the first half-mile up is arduous. Finally, when you get to the canyon bottom, the way to the Great Gallery is even but still sandy. It is not an easy place to visit. That, to me, is part of what makes it so special—the vista is hard-won, and so much a part of the canyon and the vastness of the Southwest.

While the remoteness and difficulty of the six-and-a-half-mile trail have helped protect it from the ravages of modern man, they have not been completely successful. The panel known as the Alcove Panel was vandalized a decade ago by two high school students who, while in the company of their parents and others who dissented their actions, carved their names into the panel. The vandalism garnered them a $10,000 fine, but even after some restoration work, you can still see the mar on the alcove wall from a hundred yards away. The spirit winds weep.

In 1985, I was visiting the canyon to photograph the Great Gallery for a book I was working on. I had stumbled upon the opportunity to do a book on the rock art of the Southwest and one of the photographs I had suggested for the book was of the Great Gallery. A publishing company in Golden, Colorado, was reviewing my proposal but I knew the images of the site I had wanted to capture were slightly different than those I had sent with the proposal. So, I arrived at the parking lot at dawn to get to the gallery for the morning light. The canyon walls and the painted figures on them change colors during the time of day and year. I was after morning and mid-day April light. So, I trekked to the Great Gallery, not stopping at the other panels in the canyon. When I reached my destination, I paused for reflection, for contemplation, and for permission. Only then did I begin photographing the panel. Two hours later, I sat for a short break and listened to the songs of the wind. The sounds of the canyon changed.

First, I heard their voices. Then, I saw their faces. There were three people walk-ing down the canyon. They were obviously headed directly for the gallery where I was working with my cameras. There were two men and a woman. One man was much older than the others. As a civil rights lawyer, observing human behavior is what I do for a living. I deduced that the younger man and woman were a couple and they had run into the older man on the trail. They didn't know each other but were simply hiking in together.

I rose to attend to my equipment and record additional images. When they arrived, the younger man immediately pulled out his camera, rushed to the panel, and began shooting photographs. The older man continued to talk with the woman as he pulled a 4x5 view camera out of his backpack and methodically set up his equipment. He mentioned that he wanted to propose a book of rock art. The young woman said, "I work for a publisher." He asked which one and she said, "Fulcrum Publishers." That was the company that was reviewing my rock art book proposal.

After the older man walked away and started to take photographs, I approached the young woman and said, "I apologize for eavesdropping, but I heard you mention that you work for Fulcrum Publishers. Which office?" She said, "Golden, Colorado." I said, "Hi, I'm Lawrence Baca." She gushed, "Oh, my god! I'm your editor! Your book proposal is on my desk for evaluation. Your photographs are wonderful! My husband and I come to Utah every year for vacation but we had never seen the Great Gallery. We saw your photographs and just had to come!"

Much later, the four of us hiked out

together and I called my wife immediately to report the serendipity of meeting the woman who was reviewing my book proposal in a state where neither of us lived. Two weeks later, the editor called me to say Fulcrum wanted to do the book. Then she added, "My husband wanted to know why your photographs have so much stronger colors to them than his. The detail is richer and more evocative of the panel and the canyon."

"Well," I said, "I noticed that when your husband arrived at the site he immediately pulled out his camera and started taking photographs. When I arrived two hours earlier, I stopped to listen to the spirits of the canyon and to speak with the images before I took any camera out of my bag. I left my camera equipment by the tree and stood before the panel. I thanked Creator for the beautiful morning. I thanked Creator for my life and allowing me to be in this place and sharing this day. I thanked the spirits of the canyon for allowing me

to be there before the spirit figures. I gave thanks to the ghosts of those who had placed the figures on the wall. And, lastly, I spoke to the figures themselves. I asked their permission to photograph them. I promised to honor them in all that I do with their photographs. And then I left an offering of tobacco with my thanks."

There was a long silence on the other end of the phone. I was convinced that her worldview could not accept that the figures on the wall are living entities. So I continued with, "Also, I shoot transparencies and your husband was shooting negatives. I think Velvia 50 renders the reds of the figures and browns of the canyon wall more purely than the Kodak Gold that your husband was shooting and the prints I sent you for review are custom work printed by me on Cibachrome, which further enhances the colors."

"Okay," she said, "thanks, I'll tell that to my husband."

She didn't understand a word I had said.

The "Great Gallery" absorbing April light in the afternoon.

We have a tendency to live through our cameras—to visit a site, photograph it, and leave without ever appreciating the experience. It has become a requirement of my work to contemplate first before gear is turned on. Long exposures allow me to separate myself and capture images *during* the experience.

I visited this space as a child and was captivated by the ancient carvings in the umber pockets within a stone arch. Back then a modest stone structure outlined a depression within the cliff face just below the petroglyphs. The site no longer has that spirit. That structure has now been torn down to build fire pits. The charcoal from those fires has been used to desecrate the alcoves with numerous signatures and drawings.

As an artist myself, finding commonalities in the way I represent myself on canvas and the way they represented their universe on rock is a vital component to how I represent them in the photographic medium.

Many individuals move these sensitive cover stones off of the structures' mantles to look inside, often chipping, breaking, and permanently damaging an experience of the past.

This site is no longer pristine as of late 2015. The alcove is now reported to have charcoal signatures marring the sacred images. In addition, an adjacent site is now reported to have had horse anchors drilled into the images.

An exquisitely drawn human and animal form, which likely depicts a shaman in a transformative state. The site is very fragile, situated on a thin layer of sandstone that could exfoliate at the slightest touch. It is put in increased danger by pioneered ATV trails that drive up onto the platform below the site. The increased access has led to some vandalism, which, thankfully, has faded with time. However, without action, more destruction is likely. The site is also endangered by proposed oil and gas development.

These images are often located where water touches the earth—where veins carry its essence into the pools and potholes of the canyons, occasionally completely obscuring the image through water and time.

I visited this site long before it became publicized through guidebooks and online trip reports. Then the site was mostly pristine and sections of the alcove floor were decorated with pictographs. Now, initials are carved over the rock art and the paintings on the floor have been robbed from the site.

Nature as a Stimulus for Rock Art Imagery

Lawrence Loendorf

Lawrence Loendorf is an internationally recognized scholar and archaeologist who specializes in rock art studies. He is the recipient of many awards, including the Klaus Wellman Award for distinguished service in rock art by the American Rock Art Research Association (2007); the University of North Dakota Recognition Award for Outstanding Teaching, Research, and Service (1993); the Alexander Griggs Award for Outstanding Service in Historic Preservation by the City of Grand Folks (1991); and the Lydia and Arthur Saiki Award for Undergraduate Excellence in Teaching (1983). He has also written and contributed to numerous books, monographs, and articles, as well as being a regular and highly recruited public lecturer. Loendorf is currently the president of Sacred Sites Inc., a non-profit dedicated to the protection and preservation of North American rock art sites. More about this and his work can be found at www.sacredsitesresearch.com.

Throughout the research I have undertaken at rock art sites, I have been a strong advocate for a more complete study of the entire site (Loendorf 2008). Too often, a researcher sees only the images on the wall and misses the information in the site setting that can be more important than the art itself.

In some cases, the natural setting of a site or some component of it can act as stimulus for the images at the site. For example, on a project to record the rock art sites in Canyon del Muerto, Arizona, we discovered a painting that was almost certainly a reproduction of a porcupine. It was high on the canyon wall but, without question, the figure had an excellent likeness to a porcupine and we all remarked that it was the most obvious reproduction of such that any of us had ever seen.

Several years later, I was traveling through Canyon del Muerto in the winter when the leaves were off the trees. As we rounded a corner in the canyon, someone noticed a porcupine up in one of the cottonwood trees. So we stopped to take photographs and noticed a half dozen porcupine nests in the trees, including several that were active with porcupines crawling around them. Standing there, I realized that this was the same place where we had recorded the painting of the porcupine on the rocks. I was shocked by the correlation.

Later that day, we stopped at Antelope House where Ben Teller and his Navajo family have lived for generations. I asked Ben what he knew about the nesting porcupine site and he told me that porcupines have always been found at that place in the canyon. Other rock art on the porcupine site indicates that the panel dates to Pueblo II times. This suggests that porcupines have been nesting at that location for at least a thousand years.

I have also noted similar correlations between animal habitation and corresponding rock art depictions at other locations. In the bottom of Picketwire Canyon in southeastern Colorado, there is a petroglyph of a snake biting the leg of a deer. A biologist pointed out that there is an active rattlesnake den in the canyon adjacent to the petroglyph. Similarly, at another site, an excellent petroglyph reproduction of an eagle is found west of Lander, Wyoming, where eagles nest on the same cliff wall.

The rock art does not just correlate to animals, it can correlate to other environmental features. For example, researchers are finding petroglyphs of flowers similar to the ones that grow near the panel (Hernbrode and Boyle 2013; Loendorf et al 2012) or medicinal plants like *Datura spp.* and *Nicotiana spp.* , whose neurological effects and proximity played a role in the creation of the images (Boyd 2003; Loendorf et al 2012). Given these examples, I am certain that researchers miss important information by ignoring the setting of the site while focusing on the rock art in isolation.

Sometimes there are factors other than the local fauna and flora that stimulate the content of a rock art panel. At a site in the Bighorn Mountains of Wyoming, Laurie White and I recently recorded a large figure that has the body of a human with the head and horns of a buffalo. When we stood back to view the overall context of the site, we noticed that the outcrop in which the petroglyph is situated appears to represent a buffalo emerging from the ground. It is made apparent by a protrusion of limestone that resembles a buffalo head in addition to a textured rock surface that has cavities and folds that mirrors the hide of a buffalo.

Similar figures are made on buffalo-like protrusions of rock at localities across the Great Plains. These figures have rib lines that are created within the buffalo-shaped rock face (Loendorf 2008).

From my experience as a rock art researcher, I advise you to consider the relevancy of the environmental setting and associated archaeological sites entirely, because the remnants left behind by prehistoric humans reflect their relationships to the landscape (Loendorf 2008). Researchers and visitors should resist the impulse to focus exclusively on the rock art figures themselves and embrace these factors as a part of a bigger picture.

Flowers are uncommon in prehistoric art and exceptionally uncommon in the Archaic-era painted traditions found within Utah. This pictograph allows us to see the associated landscape through the eyes of the artisan.

Sacred datura (*Datura wrightii*) played a critical role in shaping prehistory. As a hallucinogen, it was a vital part of ritual, ceremony, and also in the creation of art. Many rock art sites are situated in areas where this plant grows in abnormally high quantities.

Vibrant paintings, likely from a Numic-speaking individual, above ephedra shrubs. The paintings are now endangered by oil and gas development.

Fragments of pigment remain on several portions of this fragile rock face, reminding us that there was once an extensive mural painted above this structure that has collapsed under natural causes.

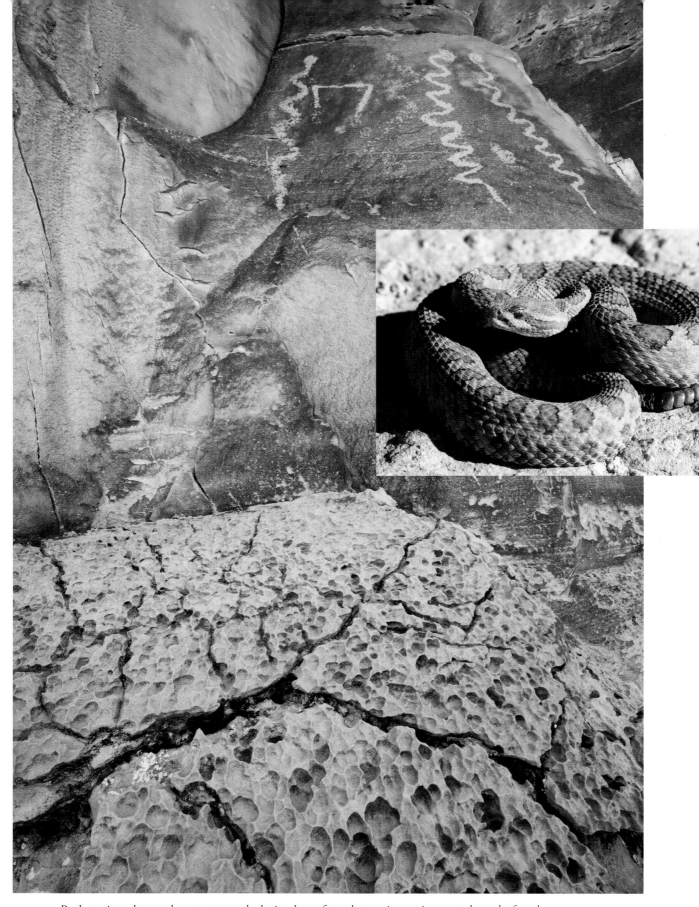

Rock art sites where snakes are commonly depicted are often where active nesting grounds can be found.

Images have become more whimsical, and yet still remarkably beautiful in the Ute's stylistic evolution.

Apparitions of time staring back from the waves of salmon red sandstone.

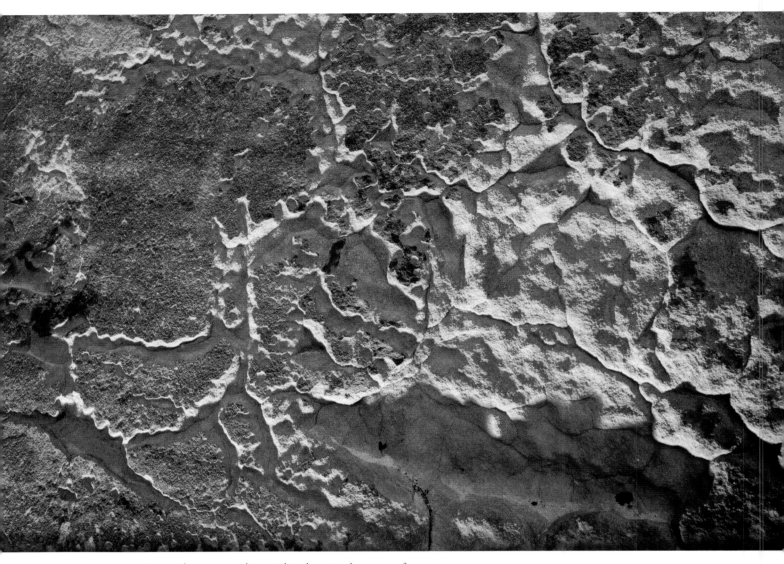

A carved canine vanishing within the natural patterns of stone.

The integration of natural features (such as nodules, cracks, and niches) adds another layer of dimension to the ancient images.

Intrusions and Delusions

Jonathan Bailey

Jonathan Bailey is an artist devoted to protecting cultural resources and the wild landscapes they inhabit. He has covered thirty thousand miles of Utah's backcountry on foot, exploring the art and minds of the people that lived there hundreds to thousands of years ago. He preserves the largest collection of photographs of San Rafael Swell rock art in the world and one of the largest collections of Utah rock art photographs internationally. His award-winning work, in both art and conservation, has been featured throughout the world in well-known journals, books, newsletters, magazines, and television shows. His work can be found at www.baileyimages.com.

It emerges like a serpent from a womb within the earth—a large sandstone spine crested with an elliptical head staring down at the confluence of two bodies of water. This space has been a veritable altar for generations as a symbol of fertility, birth, and rebirth. The faces of stone are neatly decorated with carvings from many ages, each detailing endearing images of copulation, childbirth, regeneration of plant/animal life, and successful hunting.

On the winter solstice, the sun penetrates a small chamber on the west side of this panel, extending a shadow that anchors itself with a carved rainbow while separating a male and female engaged in intercourse. This day is ascribed with connotations of regeneration and fertility as the days grow longer and more profitable.

Below this site, two creeks converge into a singular body—the intercourse of two systems of life and power, symbolically

and physically inclined to fertility (Slifer 2000). This profound interaction between the landscape and its rock art has been severely impacted by current-day irrigation projects. One of these water sources, Rochester Creek, was permanently extinguished, permanently destroying the meaning, intent, and connotations of the rock art imagery at this site. It, in combination with historic and current-day vandalism, has led to overwhelming site degradation at what is one of the most significant tourist attractions within Utah's canyon country. The site has been tormented with numerous proposals for development as well as a dramatic, sudden increase in vandalism in 2015.

Bits and pieces of the cultural landscape remain: its symbols, position in space, alignment to astronomical features, and plant life associated with many panels in the region, like ephedra and Rhus trilobata. However, due to the destruction of its cultural context, we can't experience all of these elements collectively as the artist intended. If we didn't have records of Rochester Creek, we would have never known it to have existed. No amount of documentation can or has captured this site in its natural and undisturbed state. These images are placed within complex systems that we may never fully grasp and may never get an opportunity to fully appreciate. With development projects, sites may only be granted a one-hundred-and-fifty-foot buffer (or about a one-quarter-mile buffer for sites eligible for the National Register) from newly developed roads, oil rigs, or other intrusions to the space. Considering the cumulative impacts of the development in cultural landscapes, the protections granted for cultural resources are beyond insufficient.

It comes down to multiple use—a phrase that, if you spend enough time in public land meetings, you'll learn to translate as "unchecked exploitation." The landscape itself is not a use, nor is the act of preserving it. Protecting the irreplaceable cultural and wilderness values of a landscape is the rightful suspension of incompatible uses with substantial resources ubiquitously greater than any economic, industrial, or corporate benefit. Often, the current or proposed uses of a landscape that adversely impacts cultural landscapes would not be in effect if the laws and regulations that are in place were observed. This legislation was founded upon compromises made by both parties prior to their enactment and should not be further compromised simply because these laws were not adequately enforced. Furthermore, the cumulative and provoked impacts (like the increased access and vandalism provoked by oil and gas infrastructure) are often ignored as a

critical part of the decision making process. The hundred-and-fifty-foot buffer and the annihilation of the complete and pristine cultural landscape, then, becomes the "multiple use" and the "compromise."

The outlook for our deep heritage is grim. Vandalism is increasing rapidly; people are climbing on, pulling down, and dismantling prehistoric structures; off-road vehicles (ORVs) are illegally pioneering trails up to rock art imagery, over artifacts, onto bedrock rock art panels, and through burial sites; and oil and gas and other forms of development are ravaging the landscape virtually unchecked, destroying the experience, revoking its scientific integrity, increasing access, and furthering most of these other issues. Even with the problems that could be addressed without special management labels, the Bureau of Land Management field offices are too critically underfunded to protect, manage, or have any knowledge of their cultural resources.

There are forms of preservation available to archaeological sites but they are not equipped to handle the vastly expanded impact of over-visitation, social media, and widespread location disclosure. We have seen it illustrated before—National Monument designations that provided protections but generated severe impacts from tourism and visitation. More inconspicuous methods of preservation, like National Conservation Areas, on the other hand, may still permit oil and gas development depending on how they are written. Even in Areas of Critical Environmental Concern (ACECs), people are chiseling out rock art images, burning habitation sites, and pioneering ORV trails over artifacts without retribution or management. Furthermore, the publicity generated during any public land dispute involving cultural resources is virtually inevitable whether protections are garnered or not. Look at Nine Mile Canyon, for example. A paved road now resides a hundred and fifty feet or less from many world-class rock art sites and yet the conflict has activated abnormally high impacts from visitation and vandalism. Some of these examples include: the Owl Panel, which was vandalized in 2015; the First Site, which has been repeatedly vandalized annually; and the Pregnant Bison, which was vandalized in 2014. In other words, proposals for development bring about the death of place regardless of the development's approval or denial. In most cases, the authorization of development will only proliferate multiple issues and threats, pressuring archaeologists, artists, and conservation/research non-profits to cautiously dissent. We desperately need cultural-resource-specific conservation methods to fulfill their unique characteristics and atypical requirements.

Signing petitions and griping on social media won't do the trick anymore (if it ever has). First and foremost, it is apathy that plagues the Southwest. We still have a vast record of prehistory that remains pristine but critically endangered. However, many choose inaction over action—innocence over responsibility. Ultimately, we will need to draw the line. As Edward Abbey once wrote, "wilderness needs no defense, only defenders." As I see it, if we have the time to visit these sites, we have the time to make an effort to preserve them. It is quite possible that land managers and decision makers won't make an effort to preserve some of the last pristine and remote wilderness areas and cultural resources in North America, but it is our obligation to make them, at the very least, accountable for their role in the preservation or loss of our heritage.

The alignment of light and shadow to the Rochester Creek Petroglyph site during the winter solstice. This fertility shrine has been permanently damaged by the loss of Rochester Creek, which no longer flows near the site, losing its connotation to fertility (the union of two water courses) that played a critical role in the site's placement in the landscape. The site is now endangered by proposed oil and gas development.

One of numerous fertility scenes altered by the loss of Rochester Creek. Not only has the context been destroyed, but this site also has seen an influx of vandalism, such as carved names, drawings, and initials, in the years of 2014 and 2015. The site is now endangered by proposed oil and gas development.

Muddy Creek as it meets Rochester Creek, which has now been drained entirely for irrigation. This landscape is now threatened by oil and gas development.

Although natural, this stunning panel of paintings is slowly eroding from the sandstone cliff. Fragments of the images have spalled since the 1980s. The entire panel is at risk of collapsing under its own weight. Many contemporary Native American tribes believe that this natural process should not be inhibited, that all traces of human occupation should eventually return to the earth.

Above the doorway of this structure, an impression of a small baby footprint can be seen in the mortar.

Crayon-like images painted to contour to the natural spalling of the cliff wall.

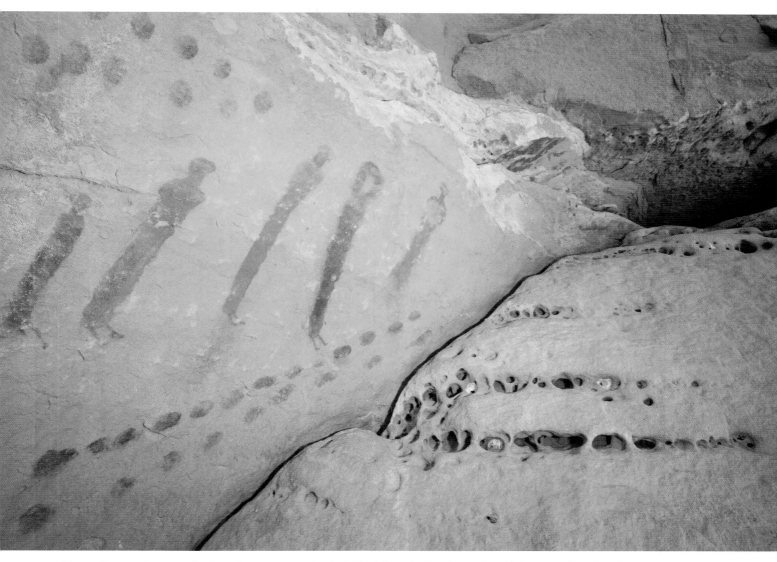

The small spots of pigment slowly evolve into mammals which bleed from the face during the transformation from bipeds (human forms) to quadrupeds (desert bighorns and canines).

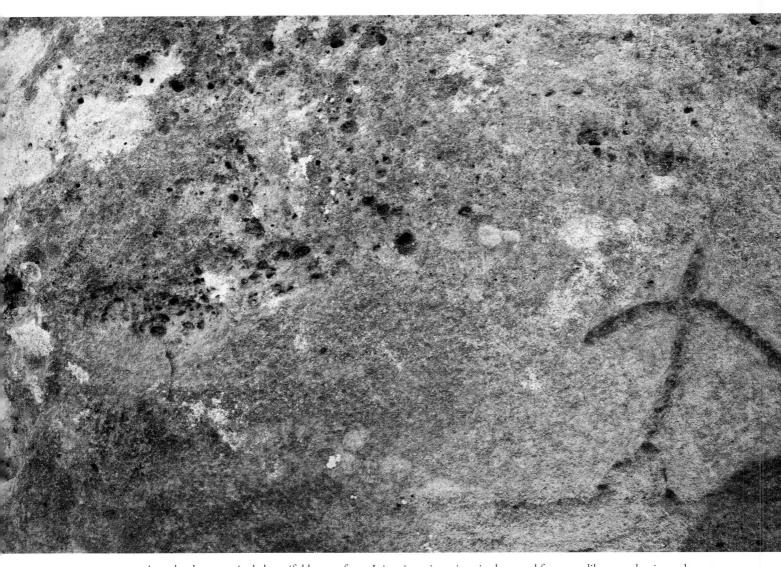

A modest but stunningly beautiful human form. It is enigmatic, unique in shape and form—unlike any other image known in Utah—and also visibly older than Desert Archaic petroglyphs carved onto an adjacent face.

Poison ivy chokes a lung-like passageway into a chamber consecrated by hunter-gatherers as well as agriculturalists. The tunnel leads below the bedrock into a single room adorned with these paintings, which guard a shallow pool of water.

The symbol of three figures holding hands is very common but its meaning is distant—lost through hundreds of years of cultural vacancy. These images are situated above a maze—a pathway one has to *know* to access its location high on the cliff rim.

Hands designating the uniqueness of its place on the span of a natural bridge that carries monsoon waters into the canyon below.

Although this site requires special permission to access, stone beads and ceramics were stolen from caches adjacent to these images.

Subtle and Obscure Little Outposts

Greg Child

Greg Child is an award-winning writer, rock climber, and mountaineer who has made numerous notable ascents including Everest and K2, and has also authored several books, including Thin Air: Encounters in the Himalayas, Over the Edge, Postcards from the Ledge, Mixed Emotions: Mountaineering Writings of Greg Child, *and* Climbing Free *with Lynn Hill. He has also written for numerous magazines, including* National Geographic, Outside, Climbing, Rock and Ice, *and* Men's Journal. *In 1980, Child moved from Australia to North America to follow in the footprints of the ancients. Recently, he was a part of a team that officially traversed the Comb Ridge—a 120-mile escarpment of sandstone covered with the traces of the Ancestral Puebloans—for the first time.*

The grand and ornate rock art panels justly get all the attention, but I've always been attracted, almost as much, by the subtle and obscure little outposts of ancient art. Case in point: On a summer day a few years ago, I went for a day hike at a place riven with canyons and outcrops of sandstone on the northern-most fling of the Ancestral Puebloan empire. I'd been hiking for hours, the sun had throttled up to full bore, and the canyon was not giving up much water, or rock art, or ruins. It started to occur to me that this might be one of those barren zones, either of little use to ancient people, or a buffer zone between different people—one of those no-man's lands, where Fremont in the north and the southern clans either intersected, or kept their distance from one another. While that

sort of place frequently turns up nothing to see, and ends up just being a parched hike and a shoe full of blisters, it can still bear fruit—if the notion of "less is more" turns you on.

I was feeling withered by the sun and decided I better get out of it and siesta under some wave of rock up above the canyon floor, before calling it quits and shuffling back to the truck. Summer in southeast Utah comes with a bite and you have to be willing to feel those solar fangs on the back of your neck and calves, but this was more than enough for even my leathery skin, so when I spied a jumble of rock that offered a cool crevice and a capstone, I slid into it.

There was enough room in there to sit comfortably cross-legged, and for me to reach out left and right with my hands.

Over my head was a roof of rock. In the heat, this slot was like a cooler, while in rain, I could shelter from even the worst thunderstorm. I'd chill out in here for half an hour, I decided, before retracing my path.

As I sat there in a pleasant mental void—just sitting, having no need to do anything or even think anything in particular—I saw in the pebbly detritus that made up the floor of the shelter, a few flakes of tan and red chert. It was the first trace of humanity I had seen all day, and it was the sort of hint of the ancients that is found absolutely everywhere in the ancient heartlands, but today in this fringe land it stood out like a neon light on a lonely road.

I realized that somebody else had hunkered down in this dismal crevice. Maybe some solitary wanderer who'd felt just as cooked as me, and had crawled in to get out of the sun. Was that person looking for something to eat, sign of animal to hunt, exploring for another canyon with a waterhole where a clan might scratch out a living and build a home? That person had, I guessed, squatted exactly where my backside was planted. To pass the time that traveler had worked the edges on a projectile point, leaving those castoff flakes. Looking more closely at the dirt floor I saw a palm-sized white pebble that had been cracked to form a point. I picked it up and found that it nestled in my hand neatly, like a pen.

Maybe this was used to scratch a message into the rock?

By this time, my eyes had adjusted from the harsh glare of sun to the shadows, and I looked at the smooth face of the boulder directly in front of me. There it was: a series of fine lines and curves etched lightly and quickly, but not masterfully, to form a likeness of the ubiquitous bighorn sheep. Crude, obscure, hidden so well that I knew I'd never find it again even if I wanted to, unimpressive to the point that I probably never mentioned the find to anyone else, this glyph of a critter made centuries ago nevertheless made the entire day memorable.

That person—man or woman or child, who could know—had shared with me the need for a shelter from heat or storm, had idled some time like me, and had scrawled what was on his or her mind onto the rock. Maybe the sheep was the quarry that day, maybe by etching that sheep it would summon it forth from the spirit and dream realm to reality, or maybe simple boredom inspired the glyph.

The little traces in the desperate places can connect with our feelings as intensely as the impressive sights of Chaco or Mesa Verde. In fact, I would rather return to that place to try and find the bighorn glyph again, and maybe stumble across more from that solo wanderer, than rub shoulders with the crowds who flock to those ancient cities.

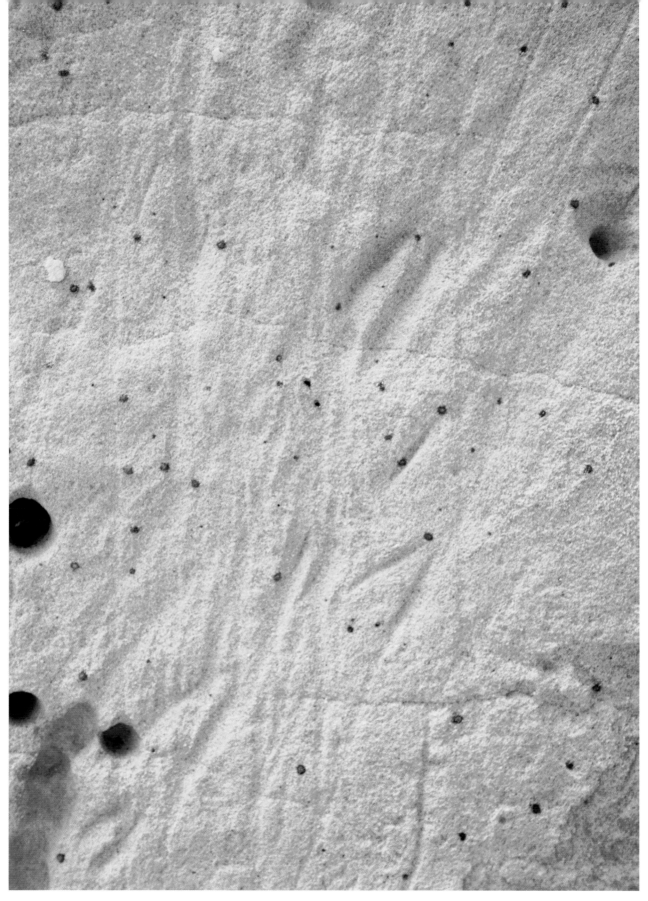

Intricate lines and drilled holes gracing the surface of sandstone in a remote shelter.

Incised lines slowly evolve into distinguishable and beautifully shaped forms.

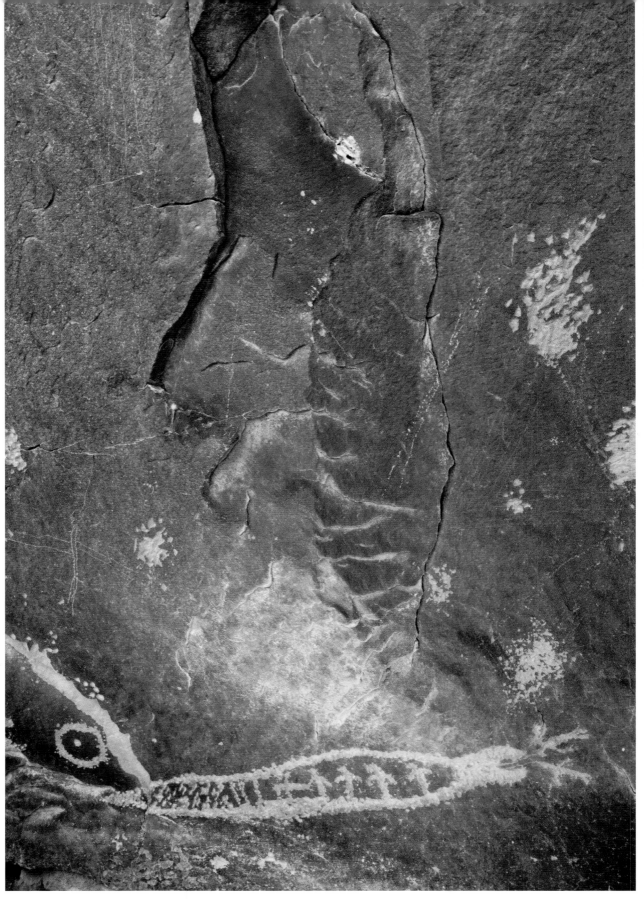

A highly unusual depiction of a serpent siphoning human figures into its stomach.

Roots grow out of the feet of a human, rooting itself to its place in an alcove with abnormal and spectacular acoustical properties.

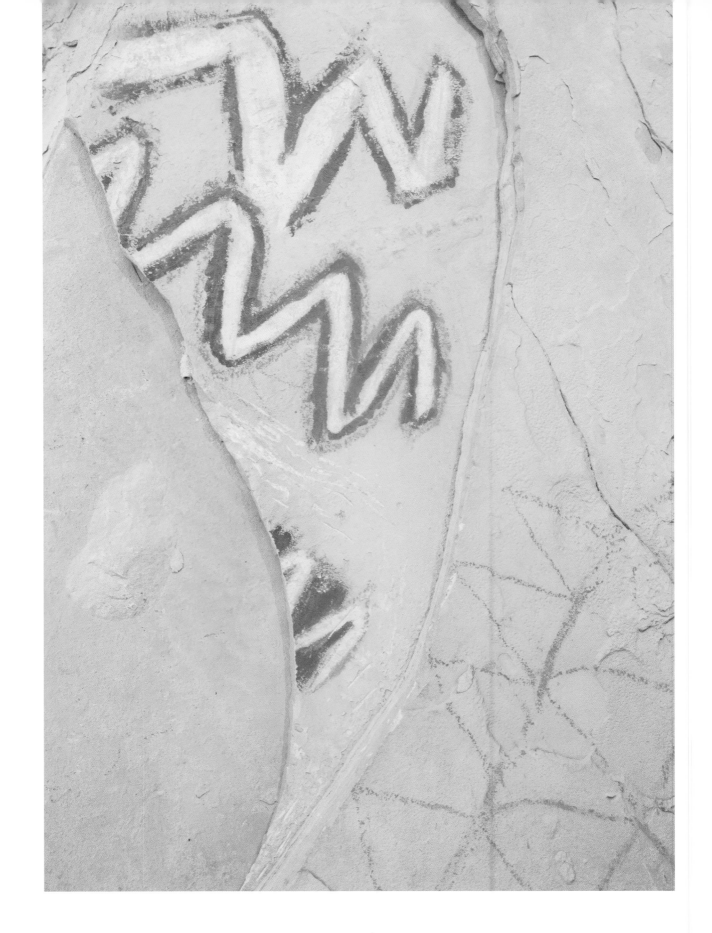

A Vanishing Act: The Endangered Rock Art of the Western United States

Jonathan Bailey

Jonathan Bailey is an artist devoted to protecting cultural resources and the wild landscapes they inhabit. He has covered thirty thousand miles of Utah's backcountry on foot, exploring the art and minds of the people that lived there hundreds to thousands of years ago. He preserves the largest collection of photographs of San Rafael Swell rock art in the world and one of the largest collections of Utah rock art photographs internationally. His award-winning work, in both art and conservation, has been featured throughout the world in well-known journals, books, newsletters, magazines, and television shows. His work can be found at www.baileyimages.com.

I walk onto a motionless plaza of indigo—a landscape intoxicated by the penetrating glance of a winter night—following the subdued reflections in a varnished carpeting of stone. Dropping off the edge, I enter a chamber—a womb within the earth itself. Moccasin tracks cover its ceiling, each painted carefully as if entering the alcove in procession. When I had visited this site a year earlier, the site had been undisturbed, obscured by an inconspicuous mantle of sandstone, hidden from tourists probing adjacent cliff lines in search of a rock art site that had recently been published in a guidebook. Now, the five-foot shelter wall is dismantled to the floor, the walls thick with carved initials, names, and dates of their desecration. The spirit of place no longer resides here.

This site isn't alone. It is part of a system—a trend—of the destruction of our past. Within three years, cases of vandalism have grown immeasurably and substantially. If continued, our past may not be a part of our future.

There is a palpable correlation between the destruction of rock art and public visitation. Between social media, blogging, trip reports, guidebooks, and other electronic modes of sharing sensitive rock art locations, the general public is accessing areas that would have been unimaginable a few years ago. Within months it seems, these newly disclosed site locations are often vandalized.

As public interest in rock art imagery grows, greater damage is done by those who disclose the locations to strangers. These are not objects to trade or give away. It is simple. If you can't trust someone with your credit card number, you shouldn't trust them with priceless and irreplaceable pieces of our past.

It becomes an issue with an interesting juxtaposition. Without any knowledge of our cultural resources we can't preserve them from development. With special land management proposals, which can add a layer of protection for cultural landscapes, there is always an increased public awareness that may lead to vandalism.

Doing a book of this weight is precarious. This book shares images of many sites that few have ever seen. By publishing these images, the awareness of these sites will increase. This is carefully mitigated by removing general locations from the images. Photographs were carefully selected to show features within the interior of the cliff face that cannot be traced using satellite imaging. Further, many of these images were selected with restricted public access in mind. Several of the images herein are located on tightly secured private lands, which, under normal circumstances, cannot be accessed by the general public. Farmers, ranchers, and other property holders have granted special permission to publish photographs of these sites for this project.

With that in mind, the majority of pristine and endangered artworks are found on federally managed public lands. They desperately need your help and stewardship! However, I chose to include fewer images of these sites simply as an added layer of protection against vandalism and unethical visitations.

These problems, collectively, are without a single solution. Education, confidentiality of locations, harsher laws, and the enforcement of those laws need to be actively employed if we desire to lessen the impact from vandalism. Similarly, both federal and state land management agencies need a more informed and educated approach in managing rock art sites and their context within the landscape when dealing with development like oil and gas. Not only does development damage the associated cultural landscape, but it also facilitates access to sensitive cultural areas with newly developed roads, provoking additional vandalism from local residents and tourists.

The preservation of cultural resources isn't simply a matter of good ethics. Damaging, obstructing, defacing, or robbing any prehistoric feature is a serious federal crime. In order to protect these resources, we ask you to never touch, tamper with, deface, obstruct, repair, or apply anything to the rock art imagery (including water). Furthermore, please use great caution when disclosing sensitive rock art locations to friends/family, or when publishing photographs online. Sensitive rock art locations can be disclosed and put in severe danger if you publish photographs or a series of photographs with contextual landscape features. Rock art images are a sacred resource of our past. Please protect them diligently and treat them honorably.

This site was destroyed in 2014 and further damaged in 2015. The structure that once stood here was torn down and the walls are now scarred with numerous initials. It is also facing threats from oil and gas development.

It only takes one individual to destroy a site. The spirit of place at this location was extinguished by a single group in the 1930s. Oil and gas development threatens to damage the site further.

Numerous bullet holes scar the face of these images.

When a site has been destroyed beyond repair and is seeing regular damage, the best and most effective option is to develop the site for public visitation. These sites can educate individuals on etiquette and appropriate site visitation.

By paving Nine Mile Canyon and increasing access, issues of vandalism have increased astronomically.

The development of oil and gas induces a proliferation of access roads that not only destroys the cultural landscape, but also provides greater access to sensitive archaeological sites, putting them at a greater risk of vandalism. This oil field in particular is to blame for a sudden upsurge of infant deaths and stillborns, likely caused by the obscene pollution produced by these fossil fuel feeding zones in the Uinta Basin. Within adjacent towns, the air is now difficult to breathe and particularly heavy with pollutants (Knox; Moulton, 2015). Photograph © Jane Pargiter, EcoFlight.

Behind the Photographs

There are lessons to be learned from light. It can move, shape, and elevate our reality into something entirely boundless. Everything from sight to color is shaped by bodies of light gracing the earth from deep distances beyond our grasp.

I experience the prehistoric peoples similarly. Their lives, beliefs, and identities are present within my existence but remain distant and, at times, intangible. As an artist, I can relate to these ancient images and people through sharing experiences. Despite the gap in time, the places they experienced and the visions of their lives can remain mostly unchanged through isolation and secrecy.

I developed a passion in fine art photography to tell and preserve the stories of the old ones—the individuals and families that connected deeply with the natural forces that governed their lives. I wanted to peel back the fabric of time to highlight, not only our connection to our deeply rooted past, but also our own role within wild landscapes.

These stories were best told by experiencing their lives and the vestiges of their existence, such as their rock art, artifacts, and structures. I chose to walk through the landscape with nothing more than I could carry and often with footwear akin to those utilized by the ancients. I chose to climb unassisted to seemingly impassable ledges that were, at times, a few inches wide, slanted, and several hundred feet above ground level. These were the lengths necessary to experience the landscape and the progression to cultural sites in a manner similar to how the original artisans and architects conceived them. It isn't without danger; in 2013 a five-hundred-pound rock dislodged from an upper cliff line while I was exploring a ridge in central Utah, which proved to be without rock art, structures, or any sign of prehistory. The boulder collided into me, ripping flesh from my leg, sending me down twenty feet of jagged rock, and narrowly missing both my head and a major artery within my leg.

In addition to thirty thousand miles of on-foot field experience (and the obligatory wear and tear), I find that it has been important to have a fundamental understanding of the technical and academic aspects of Native rock art and culture. Since the age of seven, I have independently studied rock art and archaeological concepts to further my understanding of how the ancient art and structures should be represented in digital photography. Although my focus is in the arts, a few of my academic contributions have been published in various science-oriented journals.

Despite my work in art and academia, the most critical and over-arching aspect of my work has always been in the conservation of cultural landscapes. For many years I have pushed against vandalism and development over dense archaeological zones within Utah as a representative for cultural resources in numerous public land initiatives and outreach programs. This work has protected thousands of cultural sites within central, eastern, and southern Utah. Also, my endless archive of high-resolution digital images, which remains as the largest photographic archive of Utah's Greater San Rafael Swell region in addition to hundreds of thousands of images within other regions throughout western America, will prove to be a valuable resource as vandalism and development destructs the remnants of the past.

As a conservation-minded artist, my photographs were taken with the utmost respect for the landscapes and cultural resources. It is an absolute requirement that the site is not impacted in any way by my presence. The images are photographed using a Canon 6D or backup 60D with various on-field lighting techniques that prevent the potential damage from on-board camera flashes or other potentially detrimental modes of acquiring an image. Furthermore, my photographs and written works are published with great caution to avoid damage through public awareness or visitation.

To me, these photographs are not a souvenir, they reflect the spirit of place translated through my experience of the site. Since the age of seven, I have spent literally every day of my life experiencing, protecting, or furthering my knowledge of the rock art and structures found in our desert landscapes. I express these notions with an atypical photographic style that reflects upon great painters—including those of prehistory—for inspiration. As a painter myself, I seek to push the photographic medium by manipulating the eye of the camera, minimizing the need for post processing. My systems are often bizarre and probably a bit eccentric, but it represents a vision of how I experienced these cultural landscapes.

To me, the photographic medium is very similar to how rock art imagery is perceived in much of the academic world. We create in the second dimension, focusing on the technical process, the gear, and the levels of editing, but we often neglect the fundamental experience of our subject. Our images become flat—entirely soulless. I seek to add dimension, to add myself, and the experience, back to the image. In doing so, I hope to illustrate the value of conserving the landscape, the heritage, and the spirit of place through a fourth dimension externalized and consolidated into something that can be held between the tips of your fingers.

Bibliography

Boyd, Carolyn
 2003 *Rock Art of the Lower Pecos.* College Station: Texas A & M University Press.
Hernbrode, Janine, and Peter Boyle
 2013 "Flower World Imagery in Petroglyphs: Hints of Hohokam Cosmology on the Landscape." *IFRAO 2013 Proceedings, American Indian Rock Art,* Volume 40. American Rock Art Research Association, pp. 1077–1092. Mavis Greer Session Editor, Peggy Whitehead Volume Editor.
Keyser, James
 2010 "Fisher's Landing Rock Art: An Evaluation of Petroglyphs at 45CL6." *Rock Art of the Oregon Country: Honoring the Lorings' Legacy,* James D. Keyser and George Poetschat, editors, pp. 35–66. Oregon Archaeological Society Press, Publication 18.
Keyser, James D., Michael W. Taylor, George Poetschat, and David A. Kaiser
 1983 *Visions in the Mist: The Rock Art of Celilo Falls.* Oregon Archaeological Society Press, Publication 17.
Knox, Annie and Kristen Moulton
 2015 "Midwife was right: Uinta Basin sees spike in infant deaths." *The Salt Lake Tribune,* Salt Lake City, UT.
Loendorf, Lawrence
 2008 *Thunder and Herds: Rock Art of the High Plains.* Left Coast Press, Walnut Creek, CA.
Loendorf, Lawrence, Miller Myles, and Leonard Kemp
 2012 "Picture Cave and Other Rock Art Sites on Fort Bliss." *Fort Bliss Cultural Resources Report,* No. 10–36, Fort Bliss, TX.
Loendorf, Lawrence, Abdullayev Rahmen, and Laurie White
 2015 "Desert Tobacco and Abstract Rock Paintings in Southern New Mexico." *International Newsletter on Rock Art,* No. 71:19–22.
Loubser, Johannes H. N.
 2002 "Tripping Along the Snake or On a Quest for Visions Forgotten: An Assessment of Selected Rock Art Sites in the Hells Canyon National Recreation Area." *New South Associates, Technical Report 963,* Stone Mountain, GA.
Miller, Jay
 1983 "Great Basin Religion and Theology: A Comparative Study of Power (Puha)." *Journal of California and Great Basin Anthropology* 5(1 and 2):66–86.
Pavesic, Max G.
 2007 "The Bonneville Flood Debris Field as Sacred Landscape." *Journal of California and Great Basin Anthropology* 27(1):15–27.
Ruiz, Larry.
 2015 *Waking the Mammoth,* Cloudy Ridge Productions, Friends of Cedar Mesa Annual Gathering. Documentary Film.
Ruiz, Larry.
 2013 *Death of Place,* Cloudy Ridge Productions. Documentary Film.
Slifer, Dennis
 2000 *The Serpent and the Sacred Fire: Fertility Images in Rock Art.* University of New Mexico Press, Albuquerque, NM.